# Test Your Reading

## Michael Dean

**PENGUIN ENGLISH**

To Judith with love and thanks

**Pearson Education Limited**
Edinburgh Gate
Harlow
Essex CM20 2JE, England
and Associated Companies throughout the world.

ISBN-10: 0-582-46905-8
ISBN-13: 978-0-582-46905-1

First published 2002
Sixth impression 2006
Text copyright © Michael Dean 2002

Designed and typeset by Pantek Arts Ltd, Maidstone, Kent
*Test Your* format devised by Peter Watcyn-Jones
Illustrations by Gillian Martin, Vince Silcock, Peter Standley and Sarah Wimperis
Printed in China
SWTC/06

**Acknowledgements**
The author would like to thank the editors at Penguin, led by Helen Parker
and Jane Durkin, for their skilful, supportive and sensitive editing.

Published by Pearson Education Limited in association with Penguin Books Ltd, both
companies being subsidiaries of Pearson plc.

For a complete list of the titles available from Penguin English please visit our
website at www.penguinenglish.com, or write to your local Pearson Education of fice
or to: Penguin English Marketing Department, Pearson Education, Edinburgh Gate,
Harlow, Essex, CM20 2JE.

# Contents

To the student   v

**Section 1: Messages**

**1**   Labels   1

**2**   Signs and notices   2

**3**   Form   4

**4**   Timetable   5

**5**   Sports results   6

**6**   Menu   8

**7**   Competition   10

**8**   Text messages   11

**9**   Notes and memos   13

**10**   E-mail: arrangements   15

**11**   Film review   18

**Section 2: People**

**12**   CV   20

**13**   Chat room   22

**14**   Lonely hearts   24

**15**   Job advertisements   26

**16**   Job application   28

**17**   Newspaper: horoscope   30

**18**   Missing people   32

**19**   Informal letter 1: exchange visit   34

**20**   Informal letter 2: letter from a friend   36

**21**   Gossip: newspaper and magazine articles   38

**22**   Biography   40

**23**   Novel 1: describing cultures   42

**24**   Novel 2: describing a way of life   44

**Section 3: Places**

**25**   Postcard   46

**26**   Youth hostel and hotel information   48

**27**   Directions   50

**28**   Holiday brochure   52

**29**   Formal letter 1: booking a holiday   54

**30**   Formal letter 2: complaint and dispute   56

**31**   Official notes   58

**32**   Room   60

**33**   Flat   62

**34**   Novel 3: describing towns   64

**35**   Autobiography: describing scenery   66

**Section 4: Things**

**36**   Advertments: for sale   68

**37**   Internet: buying and booking   70

**38**   Products: mail order   72

**39**   Clothes: mail order   74

**40**   Offers   76

**41**   Informal letter 3: describing a computer   78

**42**   Informal letter 4: describing clothes   80

**43**   Informal letter 5: letter of thanks   82

## Section 5: Fiction

| 44 | Rhymes | 83 |
| 45 | Cartoon | 84 |
| 46 | Comic | 86 |
| 47 | Jokes | 88 |
| 48 | Adventure story | 90 |
| 49 | Love story | 92 |
| 50 | Comedy | 94 |

## Section 6: Fact

| 51 | Headlines | 96 |
| 52 | Diary | 98 |
| 53 | How to survive an earthquake | 100 |
| 54 | Recipe | 102 |
| 55 | Formal letter 3: from the police | 104 |
| 56 | Newspaper story 1: events | 106 |
| 57 | Newspaper story 2: people | 108 |
| 58 | Newspaper story 3: sport | 110 |
| 59 | Encyclopaedia entry: a 20th century painter | 112 |
| 60 | Ideas | 114 |
| | Answers | 116 |

# To the student

Reading is very important to help you learn English. It is also a lot of fun. But to learn as much as you can from reading, it is important to read different kinds of English. For example, the English you need when you read a train timetable is very different from the English you need when you read a story. This book has a lot of different kinds of English.

There are six sections in the book:

**Section 1 is Messages:** In this section somebody wants to send information in writing to somebody else. There is a test on menus and another on timetables. There is also a test on text messages and another on e-mails.

**Section 2 is People:** In this section all the tests are about people, in different ways. For example, there is an informal letter between friends. There is formal English in a biography. There is a CV and a job application that you can use as models to help with your writing, as well as testing your reading.

**Section 3 is Places:** In this section, too, many different styles of English are shown, some informal and some formal. There is the informal English of a holiday postcard. There is also the formal English of a novel – like all the fiction extracts in the book it was written by me – and a formal letter of complaint.

**Section 4 is Things:** You will find some descriptive writing in this section. There are descriptions of clothes and of a computer. There are more examples of letters, including an informal letter thanking someone for a present. And there is a test about buying and booking on the Internet.

**Section 5 is Fiction:** There are many different kinds of fiction in this section, from an adventure story to jokes, a comic and a cartoon. There are also (as in other sections) examples of American and British English.

**Section 6 is Fact:** This section has different kinds of newspaper stories, an encyclopaedia entry, a recipe and advice on how to survive an earthquake.

You can read these tests in any order you like. You can do a complete section or jump about between sections. You can do all the tests with a fiction text, or all the tests with a letter text or a newspaper text, or all the tests with a formal or informal text. Or you can do the ones you like best first. Who knows, maybe you will like the others too, when you do them!

I enjoyed writing this book and I hope you enjoy using it.

Michael Dean

# 1 Labels

### a
All temperatures
All machines
All fabrics

**LIPSIL**

3–5 kg E10 size    New system

### c
**FOODZ**
est 1864 EST

**TOMATO KETCHUP**

FOODZ Number 7

e400 ml–460g

### e
**BARTONS**
*Strawberry Flavour*

**JELLY**
135g E

For best before end date see end of carton.
Store in a cool dry place.
Approx per 1/4 jelly
Cals: 105     Fat: Nil     Salt: Nil

### b
**FELINE**
With
**Chicken & Tuna**

You could win £100,000 plus a 1 in 2 chance to win a Feline prize.

### d
NEW Big Value Pack

*Jackson* **SMASH**
*Ant & Cockroach Killer*

*Kills bugs dead*
*Long term residual action*
*For use only as an insecticide*

### f
**TATSTIL**
28 tastatin tabs 40mg

Take ONE at night
Mrs Sheila Potts

**BLAKE Pharmacy**
Keep out of the reach of children

Read the labels and answer the questions.

1   Which *two* can people eat? _____

2   Which one can you eat on its own (not with other food)? _____

3   Which one is a sauce that you put on other food? _____

4   Which one is cat food? _____

5   Which one do you use to wash clothes? _____

6   Which one is for killing insects? _____

7   Which one tells you the last date you can use it? _____

8   Which *three* can be dangerous to a child? _____

9   Which one could make you rich? _____

10   Which one is for one person only? _____

11   Which *two* tell you where to keep them? _____

# 2 Signs and notices

a **All enquiries** *please go to reception*

b Self-service

c Have you got your new **ORANGE REWARD** card yet?
Get points every time you buy something.

d **BABY ON BOARD** Don't get too close

e **Tickets for today's performance only** Advance bookings at the next desk

f **NOTICE** Please make sure you have the means to pay before putting petrol in your car.

---

Signs and notices often use the imperative and negative imperative.

**Imperative**

*get points* = We want you to buy more and get points. (Advertising language)

*make sure* = Don't forget. It's more polite with the word *please*. (A warning)

**Negative imperative**

*Don't get too close* = Please don't drive close behind my car.

A stronger negative imperative uses *No*. For example, *No smoking*. *No Parking*.

First reading. Read the signs and notices and match them with the places where you find them.

1  theatre or cinema    _____

2  garage               _____

3  car                  _____

4  office               _____

5  supermarket          _____

6  restaurant           _____

Second reading. What do the signs mean? Choose a or b.

1  a) Don't go into the office without going to the reception desk first.

   b) Go to the reception desk if you have an enquiry.

2  a) A waiter or waitress will serve you.

   b) A waiter or waitress will not serve you. Get your food yourself.

3  a) There is a new card and you get points with it when you buy something.

   b) If you have enough points, you can get a new card.

4  a) Don't go near the baby.

   b) Don't drive right behind the car.

5  a) Go to this desk if you want to buy tickets for today.

   b) Go to the next desk if you have tickets for today.

6  a) Pay before you put petrol in your car.

   b) Check that you have enough money before you put petrol in your car.

# 3 Form

---

### VISITOR'S ENTRY FORM FOR VISITORS FROM NON-EU COUNTRIES

*Name:*

**1** Surname _____

**2** First name _____

**3** Date of birth _____

**4** Address _____

**5** Nationality _____

**6** Occupation _____

**7** Purpose of visit _____

*Accompanying persons:*

**8** Adults/relationship _____

**9** Ages of accompanying children _____

*Duration of stay in UK:*

**10** Date of arrival _____

**11** Date of proposed departure _____

**12** Domicile of UK citizen you will be staying with/visiting _____

**13** Relationship with UK citizen e.g. friend/business _____

---

Complete the entry form by writing the correct letter (a–m) next to the correct number (1–13).

### Sophie Smith's answers

| a | He's producing my programme on BBC TV |
| b | Smith |
| c | 125 East 60th Street, New York, USA |
| d | 11 and 16 |
| e | 4 August 2001 |
| f | 25 Fitzroy Street, Holland Park, London |
| g | TV Chef |
| h | 11 August 2001 |
| i | Sophie |
| j | husband Bob Smith |
| k | I'm doing a cookery programme on BBC TV |
| l | American |
| m | 5/7/1965 |

*Duration* means how long the person is staying in the country. It is the length of time between their *arrival* and their *departure*.

# 4 Timetable

---

**EURO EXPRESS**

### Euroexpress Timetable
London ↔ Ashford ↔ Lille ↔ Brussels (May–September)

| | | | | | | | | | | | | | |
|---|---|---|---|---|---|---|---|---|---|---|---|---|---|
| London-Waterloo | 0614 | 0653 | 0827 | 0853 | 1027 | 1123 | 1227 | 1423 | 1627 | 1719(1) | 1723 | 1827 | 1927 |
| Ashford | 0715 | 0753 | 0927 | – | – | 1223 | 1327 | – | 1727 | – | 1823 | 1927 | – |
| Lille-Europe | 0918 | 0956 | 1129 | 1151 | 1324 | 1426 | 1529 | 1721 | 1929 | 2025 | 2025 | 2129 | 2229 |
| Brussels-Midi | 1002 | – | 1210 | – | 1407 | 1505 | 1610 | 1802 | 2010 | 2106 | 2106 | 2210 | 2310 (2) |
| | | does NOT run on Sundays | | | | runs ONLY on Saturdays | | | | | runs ONLY on Saturdays | | |

Remarks
(1) 1727 on Saturdays
(2) Limited connection with domestic trains
An amended service will operate on and around the following Bank Holiday dates:
29 May, 12 June, 14 July and 28 August
Attention: There is always a minimum check-in time of 20 minutes. Customers who arrive at the terminal less than twenty minutes before the train leaves, may not be admitted on to the train.

---

Here are the travel plans of some people who are travelling on Euroexpress. Read the timetable carefully and tick (✓) travel plans that are OK. Put a cross (✗) if the travel plans are *probably* not OK.

1   Louise James is catching the 8.53 from London Waterloo to Ashford. _____

2   Jean Dupont will be on the 17.23 from London Waterloo to Brussels-Midi next Sunday. _____

3   The Robinsons hope to get the 19.27 from London Waterloo to Brussels-Midi. _____

4   Laura and Pete are travelling on the 17.19 from London Waterloo to Brussels-Midi on Saturday. _____

5   A football team from London is going from Ashford to Lille on the train leaving London Waterloo at 10.27. _____

6   Sophie Arnaud hopes to go from Lille to Brussels-Midi on the 15.29 from Lille on 14 July. _____

7   I am going from Ashford to Lille at 13.27 on Saturday. _____

8   Mr Black will be arriving at London Waterloo at 19.20 to get the 19.27 to Brussels. _____

# 5 Sports results

## FA CARLING PREMIERSHIP

| | |
|---|---|
| **CHARLTON (2) 4**<br>Hunt 10 Robinson 42<br>Kinsella 72<br>Stuart 80 (pen) | **MAN CITY (0) 0**<br>20,043 |
| **CHELSEA (1) 4**<br>Hasselbaink 31 (pen)<br>Zola 59<br>Stanic 78, 90 | **WEST HAM (0) 2**<br>Di Canio 48<br>Kanoute 85<br>34,914 |
| **COVENTRY (1) 1**<br>Eustace 41<br>*Sent off: D Thompson (Coventry) 71* | **MIDDLESBROUGH (1) 3**<br>Job 20<br>Boksic 59, 62<br>20,624 |
| **DERBY (1) 2**<br>Strupar 32<br>Burton 49 | **SOUTHAMPTON (2) 2**<br>Kachloul 15, 22<br>27,223 |
| **LEEDS (2) 2**<br>Smith 16, 37 | **EVERTON (0) 0**<br>40,010 |
| **LEICESTER (0) 0** | **ASTON VILLA (0) 0**<br>21,455 |
| **LIVERPOOL (0) 1**<br>Heskey 67 | **BRADFORD (0) 0**<br>44,183 |

Football results use these conventions:

The home team is always written first.

The scoring times are given over ninety minutes. Anybody who scored during minutes 1–45, scored in the first half. Anybody who scored during minutes 45–90 scored in the second half. Half-time scores are given in brackets.

A goal from a penalty is shown as *pen*.

The name of a player sent off is always given.

The number of people watching the game is always given.

Read the football results. Choose a or b.

**1**  When you read CHARLTON 4 MAN CITY 0, the game was played
   a) at Charlton  b) at Manchester City

**2**  In the game between Chelsea and West Ham, the player who scored first was
   a) Hasselbaink  b) Di Canio

**3**  Hasselbaink's goal for Chelsea and Stuart's goal for Charlton were different because they were
   a) the first goals  b) from penalties

**4**  The score at half-time in the game between Coventry and Middlesbrough was
   a) 1–3  b) 1–1

**5**  Thompson was sent off in the game between Coventry and Middlesbrough
   a) in the first half  b) in the second half

**6**  The number of people who watched the game between Leeds and Everton was
   a) 40,010  b) 40,100

**7**  The result of the game between Derby and Southampton was
   a) Southampton won  b) a draw

**8**  The game between Leicester and Aston Villa was
   a) a nil-nil draw  b) a win for Aston Villa

**9**  In the game between Liverpool and Bradford, Heskey scored
   a) in the first half  b) in the second half

# 6 Menu

## Dario's Dial-a-Pizza – takeaway pizza

### TEL: 021 765 951

### STARTERS

**❶**

**Garlic bread**

**£1.99**

*Topped with 100% mozzarella cheese and Dario's own tomato sauce*

**❷**

**Chicken dunkers**

**£3.49**

*6 chicken wings served with 2 dips: Barbecue and Chilli pepper*

### DARIO'S WONDERFUL PIZZAS

|  | SMALL | MEDIUM | LARGE |
|---|---|---|---|
| **❸ Original Cheese and Tomato** £5.50 | | £7.15 | £8.15 |
| *Topped with 100% mozzarella cheese and fresh sliced tomatoes* | | | |
| **❹ Full House** | £9.25 | £11.90 | £13.65 |
| *Onions, green peppers, olives, pineapple, prawns* | | | |
| **❺ Mighty Meaty** | £9.25 | £11.90 | £13.65 |
| *Onions, mushrooms, pepperoni, ham, sausage* | | | |
| **❻ Tandoori Hot** | £9.50 | £12.10 | £13.95 |
| *Thick pieces of Tandoori chicken, onions, mushrooms, green peppers* | | | |
| **❼ Vegetarian Supreme** | £8.50 | £10.70 | £11.90 |
| *Onions, green peppers, sweetcorn, mushrooms, sliced tomatoes* | | | |

Some of the names of the pizzas are words that say how good something is.

*wonderful* = fantastic or brilliant

*mighty* = physically strong; here it means 'very'

*supreme* = the best

First reading. Write the menu number (1–7) next to the correct picture.

Second reading. How much are these?

1   Garlic bread and a medium Mighty Meaty     _____

2   Chicken dunkers and a small Vegetarian Supreme     _____

3   Garlic bread and a large Original     _____

# 7 Competition

---

Address @ www.penguinreaders.com

**PENGUIN READERS**

BOOKS RESOURCES DOSSIERS E-BOOKS COMPETITIONS JOIN US    SEARCH

## COMPETITION

Write a Penguin Reader Review
2000 books to be won
10 winners every month

This is the only competition you can (1) _enter_ every month and have your story read by thousands of Penguin Reader fans all over the world!

Imagine you are a journalist working on the 'book (2) _reviews_ ' section of a new teenage magazine. The challenge is to write a review of a Penguin Reader. So choose your favourite Penguin Reader, write 250 words of your original ideas about the book and win some great (3) _prizes_ .

The competition will start on 1 January 2001 and run until 31 December 2001. Ten (4) _winners_ (five from each category) will be announced each month. Each winner will receive 'book box' prizes and have their names published along with their winning reviews on this website each month. The (5) _teachers_ of our winning students will also receive 'book boxes' as prizes.

Reviews will be judged in two separate (6) _categories_ , Junior (10–14 years of age) and Senior (15–18 years of age) and the prizes will be given in each.

All entries must be sent by post (see rules) so please download the entry (7) _form_ (pdf file) here.

PENGUIN READERS

keyword search

GO ►

- Search the Catalogue
- Email us
- View Shopping Basket
- Join us

---

First reading. Write the missing words in the correct places in the text (1–7).

| categories    enter    form    prizes    reviews    teachers    winners |

Second reading. Answer the questions with one word.

1   How many competitions are there in 2001? _1_

2   What do you have to write? A _book review_

3   How many winners are there in the Junior Category each month? _5_

4   What is given as prizes? _book-boxes_

5   Can you send entries by e-mail? _No_

# 8 Text messages

Gt 5xA 5xB 2C maths
& science Happy.
Txt yr results
asap Laura

Mirrors wrng size.
North Hotels rtnd
ALL. Pls advise
Jean

Team bus HighSt
8.30 Sat NOT Norman
Road.
Phone Jeff

Don't vst 45
BateRd am Computer
OK Go Hamptons pm.
Cmptr prblm

First reading. Match the abbreviations (1–8) with the meanings (a–h).

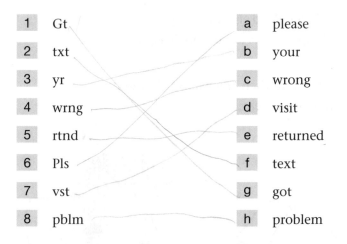

| | | | | |
|---|---|---|---|---|
| 1 | Gt | | a | please |
| 2 | txt | | b | your |
| 3 | yr | | c | wrong |
| 4 | wrng | | d | visit |
| 5 | rtnd | | e | returned |
| 6 | Pls | | f | text |
| 7 | vst | | g | got |
| 8 | pblm | | h | problem |

Mobile phone text messages have no more than sixty letters including spaces. Because of this they are nearly always written with some letters missing and some words written together.

These abbreviations can be used at any time – not only in text messages.

*asap* = as soon as possible      *Rd* = Road
*am* = in the morning      *St* = Street
*pm* = in the afternoon

Second reading. Which message is correct, a or b?

1   a) I got 5 grade As, 5Bs and 1C in maths and science. Are you
       happy? Text your results as soon as possible. Laura

    b) I got 5 grade As, 5 Bs and 2 Cs in maths and science. I'm
       happy. Text your results as soon as possible. Laura

2   a) The team bus will be in the High Street at 8.30 on Saturday,
       NOT Norman Road. Phone Jeff.

    b) The team bus was at the High Street at 8.30 on Saturday NOT
       Norman Road. Jeff phoned and told you that.

3   a) The mirrors are the wrong size. North Hotels returned ALL of
       them. Please advise them what to do with the mirrors.

    b) The mirrors are the wrong size. North Hotels returned ALL of
       them. What shall I do? Jean

4   a) Don't visit 45 Bate Road this morning. The computer there is
       OK. Go to *Hamptons* this afternoon. They have a computer
       problem.

    b) Go to Bate Road and then *Hamptons* this afternoon as they
       have a computer problem.

# 9 Notes and memos

Jo, darling
Don't be alarmed but there's been a small
accident. Tommy fell and cut his chin.
There was blood everywhere and he screamed
but it isn't too bad. I've taken him to A & E.
There'll probably be a wait. Please put the
pie on the table in the oven. And can you do
some potatoes and a salad with it? Thanks.
And darling don't go out. Please stay by the
phone in case daddy phones and then you
can tell him what's happened. Perhaps you
can get on with some homework or something.

Lots of love

Mummy

Read the note. True or false?

1    Tommy is probably younger than Jo.            _____

2    Tommy was frightened when he had the accident.  _____

3    The accident was serious.                     _____

4    Tommy is at the hospital.                      _____

5    Mummy thinks she will be home quickly.         _____

6    Mummy tells Jo to make her own dinner.         _____

7    Daddy knows about the accident.                _____

8    Jo is a student.                               _____

*A & E* = Accident and Emergency, the part of a hospital that deals with accidents.

---

## Memo

**To:** All staff
**From:** Maureen Gherkin
**Re:** Gillian Hornsey

As many of you know, Gillian Hornsey will be leaving us at the end of the month after ten years faithful service in the Accounts Department. If you have not already given money for a leaving present, please do so. May I suggest that two to five pounds would be appropriate? Also, ideas for a suitable party would be welcome. (And by suitable I do not mean a repeat of the Gorillagram who left Mavis Percy in tears when she left!)
Suitable ideas to me, please.

---

Read the memo. True or false?

1   Maureen Gherkin is leaving the Accounts Department.  _X_

2   Gillian Hornsey has worked for the same company
    for ten years.  _✓_

3   Gillian Hornsey has left the Accounts Department.  _X_

4   Nobody has given any money for a leaving present yet.  _X_

5   A party for Gillian Hornsey has not been arranged yet.  _✓_

6   Maureen Gherkin is arranging the party.  _✓_

7   Maureen Gherkin thinks a Gorillagram is a good idea.  _X_

8   Mavis Percy liked her Gorillagram.  _X_

*memo* = a business note to one or more people who work in the same company as the sender
*Accounts Department* = the department in a company that deals with money
*Gorillagram* = a person dressed as a gorilla, who is hired to give someone a surprise greeting and kiss at their birthday party, leaving party, etc.

# 10 E-mail: arrangements

## Inbox

| ! | 📎 | Subject: | From: | Sent: |
|---|---|----------|-------|-------|
| ! | | Wedding | Christine Weller | 17 July |

Dear Maureen and Clive,

David and I are so pleased to welcome Gavin into our family. I can only say that he is the son-in-law we have always wanted for our daughter, Melanie. Just to let you know about the arrangements – we have booked the wedding for Saturday 17 October, with the reception at St Jude's Church Hall, here in the village. We are inviting about a hundred people from our side and we expect you will want to invite about the same number.

With best wishes Christine (Christine Weller)

## Inbox

| ! | 📎 | Subject: | From: | Sent: |
|---|---|----------|-------|-------|
| ! | | Wedding | Maureen Higginbotham | 18 July |

Dear Christine,

Thanks for your e-mail but I wish you had asked us before booking the hall. Clive wants to invite a lot of his business friends and then there are Gavin's friends from University and my friends... Can we meet and discuss this?

Maureen

## Inbox

| ! | 📎 | Subject: | From: | Sent: |
|---|---|----------|-------|-------|
| ! | | Wedding | Clive Higginbotham | 23 July |

Dear Christine and David,

Maureen and I think that all of us should put the children first and we should forget some of the things that were said when we met at your house. I think the best answer to our problems is that *we* make all the arrangements. I have therefore booked the assembly rooms here in our city for Saturday 24 October and I have cancelled the booking you made at St Jude's Church Hall. The Assembly Rooms holds 500 people. I think we will all enjoy the wedding.

Clive Higginbotham

## Inbox

| ! | 🖉 | Subject: | From: | Sent: |
|---|---|----------|-------|-------|
| ! | | Wedding | Gavin | 24 July |

Hey Babe!

Luv ya Luv ya Luv ya. I hear the olds are planning a wedding. Oh Dear! I think we'd better tell them, don't you? Before they go ahead and book a hall and all that. Everything we wanted to avoid!!!!! Just two more weeks then Uni finishes. The flat is almost ready. Then you can come up here and we can live together at last. Can't wait!! Counting the seconds!!! Yours4ever.

Gavin

## Inbox

| ! | 🖉 | Subject: | From: | Sent: |
|---|---|----------|-------|-------|
| ! | | Wedding | Mel | 24 July |

Hey Hunk!

What's with the mobile? Is it switched off? Can't text – this is too long and too funny. Guess what?? No, don't, you'll never guess. The olds met up!!! It was a disaster. They had a huge row. I'm e-mailing them now with the news.

Luvyaloads

Mel

## Inbox

| ! | 🖉 | Subject: | From: | Sent: |
|---|---|----------|-------|-------|
| ! | | Wedding | Mel | 24 July |

Dear mum and dad and Mr and Mrs Weller,

There's no easy way of saying this but Gavin and I got married six months ago. We were going to tell you, honest. But we never seemed to have time... Sorry!

Mel

First reading. Tick (✓) the summary that has no mistakes in it, a or b.

**a** Two couples, the Wellers and the Higginbothams, both wanted to book a hall for the wedding of their children, Gavin and Melanie. The Wellers and the Higginbothams had a row about the arrangements, so Gavin and Melanie booked the wedding themselves.

**b** Christine and David Weller wanted to book a hall in their village for the wedding of their daughter Melanie to Gavin, the son of Clive and Maureen Higginbotham. But the Higginbothams thought the hall was not big enough. The Wellers and the Higginbothams had a row. The Higginbothams then booked another, bigger, hall. But Melanie and Gavin had married six months ago without telling their parents.

Second reading. Tick (✓) the person or people who ...

| | | Christine & David Weller | Maureen & Clive Higginbotham | Gavin | Melanie |
|---|---|---|---|---|---|
| 1 | had his mobile off | | | | |
| 2 | wanted to invite a hundred people | | | | |
| 3 | booked the Assembly Rooms | | | | |
| 4 | lives in a village | | | | |
| 5 | is at University | | | | |
| 6 | lives in a city | | | | |
| 7 | wanted to avoid a wedding reception | | | | |
| 8 | is getting the flat ready | | | | |
| 9 | booked the wedding for 24 October | | | | |
| 10 | told the parents about the wedding | | | | |
| 11 | booked St Jude's Church Hall | | | | |

# 11 Film review

## The Review

**a** *The Love Thing* is the latest vehicle for Grant Twiss, recently voted most attractive man in the world by *Girl Alive* magazine. The story is minimal. Twiss's character, lovable Simon, is the only one of his friends who is not married. Twiss goes to all the weddings until he eventually finds love. Will you like it? Yes, of course you will.

**b** Cameraman Pete Olnay won an award for some of the stunning shots of the Rocky Mountains in *Ben, Gin and Tilly*. Ben and Gin are dogs and Tilly is a cat. When a family leave home and leave their animals behind, Ben, Gin and Tilly travel a thousand miles across the Rockies to find them. All three animals can talk and their pet's-eye view of life is a treat.

**c** Wyatt Earp was born in Pella, Iowa. He was just old enough to fight on the Union side in the Civil War – he was fifteen. His family went to California in 1864 as part of a wagon train. He arrived in Tombstone, Arizona, in 1879 and the famous gunfight at the OK Corral between the Earp Brothers and Doc Holliday was two years later. Only Wyatt was alive after the gunfight. It's a great story and it is well told in *Wyatt*, veteran director Bob Santana's first film for ten years.

**d** As a couple they are just too good to be true. He is an award-winning scientist. She is a brilliant concert pianist, but she gave it up to look after the kids. This is America, so they are both beautiful. And their house is beautiful, even if it is haunted. But what the spirit tells Petronella (Carrie Langtry) about her husband (Barney Grable) makes her see their marriage in a new light. For one thing he tries to kill her. And I can still hear her scream. You really must see *The House on the Hill*.

Read the film reviews (a–d) then decide which film is best for which person.
Match 1–4 with a–d.

**1** **Geoff**

My hobby is the American West. I read
about the American Civil War, the
Indian Wars and cowboys all the time.
I love westerns. They're my favourite
films.

**2** **Melissa**

My idea of heaven is to go to a good
film and then a meal with about six
girlfriends. Ideally, the film should be
romantic without being too silly. And a
few good-looking male film stars always
helps!

**3** **Sandra**

I go to the cinema to be scared. I don't
like stories about everyday life. I can get
everyday life at home, thank you. I want
to be terrified, I want to scream. I like
horror films, ghost films, murder,
mystery. I don't care as long as I'm
frightened!

**4** **Reg**

Since I started watching films with my
children, I quite like kids' films. I've
always been an animal lover and if the
film has animals in it, so much the
better.

# 12 CV

**Name:** Jane Felicity Westmacott
**Address:** Top Flat, 210B Central Road, Brixton, London SW2 4EJ
**Tel/fax:** 020 7547 8947
**E-mail:** Janwest@freenet.com
**Date of birth:** 3rd June 1979

**School 1990–7**
The Charles Dickens School, Fuller Way, Gads Hill, Kent GR3 6WO
**1995:** *10 GCSEs*
English Language Grade A*    Science I Grade B    IT Grade B
English Literature Grade A    Science II Grade B    French Grade B
History Grade B    Statistics Grade B    Geography Grade B    Mathematics Grade C
**1997:** *3 A Levels*
Geography Grade C    History Grade B    English Lang and Lit Grade B
**2001:** A/S Graphic Design taken privately at Brixton Adult Education Centre

**University 1997–2000**
The University of Central England, Fissborough, near Coventry CR8 5LL
BA (Hons) in Media Studies (Upper Second)

**Work history 2000–present**
**2001–present**
Project Manager at WebUnlimited, 25 Weald Road, Guildford, Surrey GU1 4TX
tel: 01483 610781
I manage a small team that arranges and designs website advertising. We also suggest other ways that clients can earn money from their websites.

**2000–2001**
Website Designer at South London Creative Consortium, 16 Streatham Hill, Streatham SE6 7OP
tel: 020 6142 2249

**Referees:**
Claire Tremaine (my present boss)                Professor Rodney Bartlett,
WebUnlimited (above address)                Department of Media Studies,
                The University of Central England

CV = Curriculum Vitae, but the abbreviation is more usual. You send a CV when you apply for a job.

*referees* = people who will write references about the person, saying that they are suitable for a job.

*GCSE* = examination taken by sixteen-year-olds in Britain – about ten subjects usually. The top grade is A* ( = A star).

*A Level* = examination taken in three or four subjects (usually) that leads to study at University.

*A/S Level* = Advanced Subsidiary. Worth half an A Level.

*BA* = Bachelor of Arts, but the abbreviation is more usual. University first degrees are usually either BA or BSc (Bachelor of Science).

Choose the correct answer, a b or c.

1  What is Jane Westmacott's postcode?

   a) CR8 5LL
   b) GU1 4TX
   c) SW2 4EJ

2  What is Jane Westmacott's fax number?

   a) 020 5547 8947
   b) Janwest@freenet.com
   c) 01483 610781

3  Where did Jane Westmacott go to school?

   a) Brixton, London
   b) Gads Hill, Kent
   c) Fissborough, near Coventry

4  In which subject did Jane Westmacott get the best GCSE Grade?

   a) English Language
   b) English Literature
   c) History

5  Which qualifications did Jane Westmacott get before university?

   a) 10 GCSEs and 3 A Levels
   b) 10 GCSEs and 4 A Levels
   c) 10 GCSEs, 1 A/S Level and 3 A Levels

6  What is Jane Westmacott's university qualification?

   a) Media Studies
   b) The University of Central England
   c) BA (Hons) in Media Studies (Upper Second)

7  How many jobs has Jane Westmacott had?

   a) 1
   b) 2
   c) 3

8  Who are Jane Westmacott's referees?

   a) the bosses of the two companies where she worked
   b) the boss of the company where she works now and her school headmaster
   c) the boss of the company where she works now and her professor at university

9  Which jobs did Jane Westmacott describe on her CV?

   a) her present job only
   b) all her past jobs
   c) her last two jobs

# 13 Chat room

Hello out there. I am sitting on the floor in the dark. There is no furniture in this room. There is only the light of the computer. I can see the lights of the big city out of the window. I don't know anybody in this city. Is there anybody out there? – NEW BOY

Hello, New Boy. Why isn't there any furniture in the room? – WORRIED GIRL

Hi, Worried Girl. Because all my furniture is still in Scotland – where I come from. It arrives tomorrow. I came down by train a day early to visit the company where I start work next week. I had a meal in a cafe. Then I went for a walk. Except for the hour at my new office I haven't talked to anybody for three days. What are you worried about, worried girl? – NEW BOY

Oh, new boy, you sound so sad. I'm worried about my exams. It's ridiculous isn't it? I'm twenty-three and I'm worried about my exams, like a schoolgirl. What did you have to eat at the cafe? – WORRIED GIRL

What a funny question! Well, promise you won't laugh. I usually eat good healthy food. But I felt so alone here. So I had Big Joe's Fry Up. It was fried sausages, chips, bacon ... Are you hungry? – NEW BOY

Yes, I'm starving. I don't know why. I'm nervous about my exams tomorrow and I think that's making me hungry. I think I'll make a sandwich. Why don't you join me for dinner? – WORRIED GIRL

But how can I ...? Ah, I understand. OK, I'm back now. I just went to get half a sandwich that I bought on the train. I'm just eating now. Nice having dinner with you worried girl. – NEW BOY

Nice having dinner with you, too, new boy. To be honest, this is my first date for about a year. Can't remember the last time I spoke to anybody actually ... And do you know something? I feel better now. You've really cheered me up. – WORRIED GIRL

I feel better too. Really! OK. Must go. Good luck for tomorrow. – NEW BOY

Good luck to you, too. Good luck with the job. – WORRIED GIRL

First reading. Tick (✓) the correct column.

| | | New Boy | Worried Girl | both | neither |
|---|---|---|---|---|---|
| 1 | is happy | | | | |
| 2 | is hungry | | | | |
| 3 | has a computer | | | | |
| 4 | has no furniture | | | | |
| 5 | comes from Scotland | | | | |
| 6 | is starting a new job | | | | |
| 7 | had a meal at Big Joe's | | | | |
| 8 | made a sandwich | | | | |
| 9 | found a sandwich | | | | |
| 10 | hasn't talked to anybody for some time | | | | |
| 11 | felt better after the talk | | | | |

Second reading. Find words in the text which mean the following.

1   tables, chairs, armchairs, etc.     _____

2   very silly     _____

3   food cooked in a way that is bad for your health     _____

4   very hungry     _____

5   a little bit afraid about what might happen     _____

# 14 Lonely hearts

## Finding someone new

### Women seeking men

**OUTGOING**
Female, 24, brown hair, blue eyes, 5' 4", enjoys socialising, evenings in and out, seeks genuine male with similar interests for friendship/possible relationship.

**SUMMER FUN!**
Friendly, divorced female, 32, seeks tall, dark, handsome male, 35–42, for love and laughter.

**CHECK THIS OUT**
Fun, professional female, 25, enjoys keep fit, clubbing, cinema, spending time with friends, seeks man with similar outlook for friendship/possible relationship.

**A GOOD CATCH**
Easygoing, down-to-earth female, 28, GSOH, seeks fun-loving male, 27–32, for friendship, fun and romance.

### Men seeking women

**SIMPLE GUY**
Roger, 25, enjoys pubs, clubs, eating out and cinemas, seeks a female of similar age for a serious relationship.

**CHOOSE ME!**
Male, 26, 5' 8", brown hair, enjoys cosy nights in, occasional nights out, riding his motorbike, seeks female with similar interests for friendship and maybe marriage. Sudbury area.

**HIGH ENERGY**
Intelligent male, 20s, N/S, into music, discovery, the arts and life, seeks female to share life with.

**WIDE HORIZONS**
Male writer, early 40s, many interests/ambitions, considered handsome, highly solvent, wltm pleasant female, 25–45, for friendship, hopefully a relationship.

*wltm* = would like to meet  *N/S* = non-smoker
*GSOH* = good sense of humour

Read the advertisements and answer the questions.

1 Which woman gave her age, colour of hair, colour of eyes and height? _____

2 Which woman gave the most hobbies/free-time activities? _____

3 Which women gave no hobbies/free-time activities? _____

4 Which woman did not say what sort of person she is? _____

5 Which woman said what sort of job she does? _____

6 Which woman described what her man should look like? _____

7 Which woman has been married? _____

8 How many men gave their height? _____

9 How many men gave their exact age? _____

10 How many men gave the age of the woman they are looking for? _____

11 How many men said they were rich? _____

12 How many men said where they live? _____

13 How many men said something about the woman they are looking for? _____

14 How many men definitely don't smoke? _____

# 15 Job advertisements

**A**

## WE NEED DISTRIBUTORS AGED 13+ IN ALL AREAS

- - - - - - - - - - - - - - - - - - - - -

*Would you like the opportunity to earn extra cash close to home? If so we have a vacancy in our team of local distributors which would suit you. Both adults and youngsters aged 13+ are required to deliver your local free paper.*

### FOR MORE INFORMATION
### TELEPHONE 0196 – 675898

- - - - - - - - - - - - - - - - - - - - -

ALTERNATIVELY POST THE
COUPON BELOW TO:
UNIT 2 FISHER BUSINESS PARK
TAGWOOD INDUSTRIAL ESTATE
LANCHESTER LA4 7BU

**B**

## PAYROLL CONTROLLER LANCHESTER FISH

*

Must be able to work on own initiative.

*

High degree of computer literacy required.

*

Ability to develop new payroll systems an advantage.

*

### £18,000 p.a.

Write with full CV and two referees to:
Lanchester Fish
15 Collings Lane
Lanchester
LA5 8RU

**C**

**THE KINGDOM COUNTRY CLUB**
requires
**EXPERIENCED CHEF/COOK**
Must be motivated and creative with food.

**EXPERIENCED BAR MANAGER/BAR PERSON**
required full time. Accommodation available if required as part of the package (wage negotiable).
Could possibly suit couple.

**PART-TIME BAR STAFF REQUIRED**
Tel 0196 – 887323 during office hours

**D**

## SELL INJURY INSURANCE
**Previous experience NOT essential. Local area. Expenses paid. Training provided. Major international company. Excellent career prospects + package.**
### CALL 0196 436211
### FOR LOCAL INTERVIEW

**E**

**PATTISON & CO SOLICITORS**
have a vacancy for a
***PART-TIME MATURE PERSON***
to make/serve refreshments for their staff – 20 hours per week (4 hours per day) times by arrangement.
For further information telephone Di Washbourne on 0196 664433

**F**

**CARER** required for part-time hours in our nursing home. We provide high standards of care and offer an excellent working environment. For details and conditions of service contact: Petronella Hoare, Lambtons. Tel. 0196 504504

Both *package* and *conditions of service* mean hours of work, holidays and other aspects of the job outside the salary itself.

First reading. Read the advertisements and answer the questions.

| 1 | Which advertisement is advertising more than one job? | _____ |
| 2 | Which advertisement advertises the salary? | _____ |
| 3 | Which advertisements have jobs that are full time? | _____ |
| 4 | Which advertisements have jobs that are part time? | _____ |
| 5 | Which advertisements mention the person's age? | _____ |
| 6 | Which advertisement is for a job with computers? | _____ |
| 7 | Which advertisements are for people who have done the job before? | _____ |
| 8 | Which advertisements can you answer by post? | _____ |
| 9 | Which advertisement could be answered by two people together? | _____ |
| 10 | Which advertisement offers somewhere to live? | _____ |

Second reading. Match the jobs (1–8) with the job descriptions (a–h).

| | | | |
|---|---|---|---|
| 1 | distributor | a | makes cups of tea and gives them to staff |
| 2 | chef/cook | b | is in charge of the bar |
| 3 | bar manager | c | makes meals |
| 4 | bar staff | d | looks after people who are old or ill |
| 5 | payroll controller | e | sells insurance against being hurt |
| 6 | injury insurance salesperson | f | helps to calculate salaries |
| 7 | a person to serve refreshments | g | help at a bar |
| 8 | carer | h | pushes newspapers through the letter box |

# 16 Job application

26 Farleigh Road
Lanchester
LA4 6KP

Lanchester Fish
15 Collings Lane
Lanchester
LA5 8RU

20 November 2001

Dear Sir or Madam,

1  I am writing (a) _____ your advertisement for a payroll controller for Lanchester Fish in the Wessex Gazette of 19 November 2001.

2  I am (b) _____ a payroll assistant at Lanchester Tennis Club. I joined them when I left school. (Please see attached CV.)

3  (c) _____ you say you are looking for someone who can work on his or her own initiative and develop payroll systems. During the recent unfortunate illness of the payroll controller at the Tennis Club, I have had to both run the department by myself and develop new systems.

4  You also mention in the job advertisement that a high degree of computer literacy (d) _____ . Computers are my hobby and of course I use them at work at the Tennis Club. I know all the major programs on PCs and Macs and have carried out repairs to the computer system at the Tennis Club when necessary.

5  I am (e)_____ my CV with this letter.

6  I would be very happy (f)_____ if selected.

Yours faithfully,

*D Rogers*

David Rogers

This is a formal letter, so it starts *Dear Sir or Madam* and ends *Yours faithfully*. There are no contractions – for example, *I am* not *I'm*.

First reading. Write the missing words in the correct places (a–f) in the letter.

| | | |
|---|---|---|
| in your advertisement | enclosing | to attend for interview |
| is required | at present | in reply to |

Second reading. Look at the paragraph summaries (a–f) below. Match each summary with the correct paragraph number (1–6).

a  David Rogers says how his job fits the job advertisement 1. _____

b  David Rogers says how his job fits the job advertisement 2. _____

c  Where David Rogers saw the advertisement. _____

d  David Rogers wants to come to a job interview. _____

e  What David Rogers's job is now. _____

f  David Rogers's CV is with the letter. _____

# 17 Newspaper: horoscope

Read the horoscopes. There are three extra words in each horoscope which should not be there. Cross them out. The first one has been done for you.

### ARIES (March 20 – April 18)

Life has been ~~square~~ exciting lately, exciting enough even for an Aries! But from today Mercury, the planet of mind and ideas, enters a sensitive place area of your chart bringing situations that will need your care and attention. Take your time if you don't want to make no mistakes.

### TAURUS (April 19 – May 19)

Make the best of today's sudden and unsettling pleasant changes. At first it seems as though these are until a threat to your financial well-being. But look more closely and you will see long-term unpleasant opportunities which will become clearer on Thursday when your ruler, Venus, forms a superb aspect to Uranus.

### GEMINI (May 20 – June 20)

You have lately been reconsidering many areas of your life. Today, as Saturn goes retrograde, you begin for to question some of the decisions you have made. Issues come to a point head but don't be too concerned. A positive outcome can be expected of next week.

### CANCER (June 21 – July 21)

The decisions you make today have less to do with the facts and more welcome to do with how you you feel about certain situations and certain individuals. By all the means talk things over with others – and with Mercury forming a series of aspects everyone will have something to say – but in the end it is your decision.

### LEO (July 22 – August 21)

You suddenly become closer to your a friend who only recently was irritating you. Today's full moon sees you planning fruit future events with them. Stay open-minded as the suggestions that are made concerning these events are in on your best long-term interests. Even if they don't seem to be at first!

*'My horoscope says that I'll get a big surprise soon.'*

The language of horoscopes

*chart* = astrological chart – the way the stars influence your star sign

*aspect* = the position of the stars in relation to each other

*retrograde* = the planet is travelling backwards (usually a bad sign)

*Saturn, Uranus, Venus, Mercury* = planets

Horoscopes often use the present simple, (e.g. *Issues come to a head...*). The present perfect progressive is also used a lot for things that have been happening lately, (e.g. *You have lately been reconsidering ...*).

# 18 Missing people

## Have you seen these people?

### Jane Peters, aged 21

Jane was walking to college with a friend. The friend went back to her flat because she had forgotten something and Jane walked on alone. She never arrived at college and she has not been seen for the last five years. CCTV film of some shops near the college shows Jane talking to a man on the afternoon that she disappeared. None of her friends can identify the man. Several young women have disappeared in that area, and police and her family and friends are very concerned about her.

Jane is of slim build and blonde. When she was last seen, she was wearing a blue anorak, red pullover and jeans. She was carrying a green carrier bag, with her books in it.

### Arthur Sugden, aged 61

Arthur went to get a newspaper at the local corner shop and never came back. He has been missing for seven years. His wife Pru says he had problems at work but for him to just walk out like that was 'completely out of character'. It is thought that Mr Sugden had money worries and police believe he had been gambling. Mrs Sugden and the couple's daughters Sheila, now aged 32, and Jeanette, 28, appeal to Mr Sugden to come back. 'Whatever the problem is, we can put it right together,' says Mrs Sugden.

Mr Sugden is of medium build and has thinning brown hair. When last seen he was wearing a tweed jacket, grey trousers and a white shirt with a red tie.

### Richard (Dickie) Gallagher, aged 5

Last summer, Dickie Gallagher was playing on the beach on the family holiday in Corfu when he suddenly disappeared. The police searched the beach and interviewed people at nearby hotels. Coastguards searched the sea for two days after he disappeared. They believe that if Dickie had drowned the body would have been found by now. His older brother Leon, aged 12, was looking after Dickie while his parents went back to their hotel for a sleep. Dickie climbed over a wall and when Leon went to look for him he was gone. No tourists on the beach remember seeing him on his own. Mr Tom Gallagher, a driver with British Rail, has given up his job to return to Corfu. The family are preparing to sell their house to raise money to help in the search for Dickie.

Dickie Gallagher has dark hair and when last seen he was wearing black swimming trunks.

> *CCTV* = closed-circuit television-cameras that record what happens in a particular area, e.g. in the street or in a shop.
> *corner shop* = a small shop – not a supermarket
> *Corfu* = a Greek island popular with British holidaymakers

First reading. True or false?

## Jane Peters

1   Jane and her friend walked to college together.                    _____

2   Jane disappeared five years ago.                                    _____

3   Jane and her friend were on the CCTV film,
    talking to a man.                                                   _____

4   Jane is not the first person to disappear in the area.              _____

## Arthur Sugden

1   Mrs Sugden thought Arthur was coming back from the corner shop.     _____

2   Arthur's family thought he might disappear.     _____

3   Nobody knows exactly why Arthur disappeared.     _____

4   Mrs Sugden still hopes that her husband will come back.     _____

## Richard (Dickie) Gallagher

1   Dickie disappeared near his home.     _____

2   Coastguards searched the sea for Dickie.     _____

3   The last person to see Dickie was his brother Leon.     _____

4   Dickie's parents were on the beach when he disappeared.     _____

Second reading. Which of these pictures best fits the descriptions of the missing people?

**Jane Peters**       **Arthur Sugden**      **Dickie Gallagher**

1     3     5

2     4     6

# 19 Informal letter 1: exchange visit

558 Van Ness Ave
San Francisco CA 94102
tel. (415) 974-0904

Hi Uwe!

How are you? Wow, when I sit down and write to you like this, I remember so many great things – all those warm evenings sitting out in the garden of the Cafe Aigner, those times we went swimming with all your friends, the ice skating ... Say hello to everybody in Esslingen for me, especially your mom and dad. By the way, is it OK if I write to Brigitte? I have her address. I know you two go back a long way, but she's not your girlfriend is she? I just want to make sure ...

My mom says to say hello to your folks and to tell you she needs a recipe to make all those south German specialties I haven't stopped talking about. Maybe your mom could write? The recipe for Spaetzle will do for a start!

So when are you coming to San Francisco? I guess February is out of the question, and too bad because it's Chinese New Year and the celebration is really spectacular. More realistically, the Giants, our baseball team, sponsor a youth baseball camp in June. How would that work out with your vacation time in Baden-Württemberg?

It's been hard going back to school after such a great summer in Germany. Luckily, an elective in Modern Political Systems is saving my life. It is the ONLY interesting thing I am doing with my life! Oh yes, that and a program for the school radio station on classic rock. Yours truly is the star DJ.

OK, Uwe, write me soon, or e-mail if that's better for you.

Take care
Pete

American English
*elective* = a school subject you can choose to do. You don't have to do it.
*program* = British English spelling is programme (but not for computers).
*specialty* = British English spelling is speciality.

Choose the best answer, a, b or c.

1  How old do you think Uwe and Pete are?

   a) between 16 and 18

   b) between 25 and 30

   c) older than forty

2  Which of these tell you that the letter was written by an American?

   a) Chinese New Year + it's been hard going back to school

   b) the recipe for Spaetzle + say hello

   c) school radio + electives + write me

3  In which month was this letter written?

   a) probably in June or July

   b) probably in September

   c) probably in February

4  When was this letter written?

   a) probably a short time after Pete's visit to Esslingen

   b) probably a long time after Pete's visit to Esslingen

   c) probably the day he arrived back in San Francisco

5  Was this Pete's first visit to Esslingen?

   a) Definitely, yes.

   b) We don't know but probably yes.

   c) We don't know but probably no.

6  Have Pete's parents met Uwe's parents?

   a) Definitely, yes.

   b) We don't know but probably yes.

   c) We don't know but probably no.

7  Has Uwe ever been to San Francisco?

   a) Definitely, yes.

   b) We don't know but probably yes.

   c) We don't know but probably no.

8  What does Pete think about Brigitte?

   a) He thinks she is Uwe's girlfriend but he likes her.

   b) He hopes she is not Uwe's girlfriend because he likes her.

   c) He knows that she has known Uwe for a long time and she was his girlfriend.

# 20 Informal letter 2: letter from a friend

> Linwoods
> 12 East Point Road
> Fannie Bay
> Near Darwin
> Australia
>
> 25 October

Dear Emily,

Touch wood, things are not too bad for me at the moment. I still have that cough that Dr Maclaren isn't interested in and my back hurts when I sit too long. The leg problem is much better, though.

Our big excitement here recently was visitors from England. A rather pretty young girl came to the home, with no warning, and said she was my great nece. All the nurses made a big fuss of her and all the other people in the home wanted to know who she was. Unfortunately, I couldn't tell them. Anyway, she is a charming girl called Carol who is backpacking around Northern Territory with a friend (also a girl, thank heavens). This friend was a bit miserable. The two of them had come in the rainy season and she kept complaining that it was raining. Silly girl. Her name is Selina, which is a silly name, too.

Carol and Selina did all the things that tourists do here. They went to Kukudu National Park and Jim Jim Falls. They took the most wonderful photographs which they were kind enough to come back and show me. Carol caught a barramundi (a local fish) and as she gave me two copies of the photograph, I'm sending one to you. Apparently they had an Aborigine guide. That other girl, Selina, kept asking me about the Aborigines, as if everything that has happened to them was my fault.

But Carol was quite interested in my stories about Darwin in the old days. I lived through the bombing in World War II, you know. I know you Londoners think London was the only place that was bombed, but it wasn't. And I nearly died when the cyclone hit us at Christmas in the 1970s. I told Carol all about that. One of the ladies who lives here had some photographs of that, too. That was nice, but one woman, Mrs Apthorpe, wouldn't leave us alone when Carol was here. We don't get many young people here, I know, but Carol had come to see me, not Mrs Apthorpe.

Well, I must stop now. It's time for my afternoon medicine and then I must have a nap. I hope you are keeping well.

Love Mabel

Choose the best answer, a, b or c.

1   How old do you think Mabel Green is?
    a) between twenty and thirty
    b) between thirty and fifty
    c) older than sixty

2   What do you think Mabel Green's main interests are?
    a) her health (how she is feeling) and her memories
    b) tourism in the Northern Territory
    c) the Aborigines

3   Where do you think Mabel Green lives?
    a) in her own home
    b) in a nursing home for old people
    c) in a house with Mrs Apthorpe

4   Where does Emily live?
    a) We don't know.
    b) Probably in Northern Territory but we don't know.
    c) Probably in London but we don't know.

5   Who does Mabel Green like?
    a) Dr Maclaren
    b) Mrs Apthorpe
    c) Carol

6   Who does Mabel Green dislike?
    a) only Dr Maclaren and Mrs Apthorpe
    b) Dr Maclaren, Mrs Apthorpe and Selina
    c) Dr Maclaren, Mrs Apthorpe, Emily and Selina

7   Has Mabel Green lived in Darwin since she was a young woman?
    a) We don't know.
    b) We don't know but probably yes.
    c) We don't know but probably no.

8   What does Mabel Green think has happened to the Aborigines?
    a) good things
    b) bad things
    c) some good and some bad things

*Aborigines* = The people who lived in Australia before the Europeans came in the eighteenth century.

*cyclone* = a very strong wind. Cyclone Tracey destroyed most of Darwin (the state capital of Northern Territory) on Christmas Eve 1974.

*rainy season* = The Northern Territory has a tropical climate and it rains, sometimes heavily, from November to April.

*backpacking* = travelling cheaply over a long distance, usually by young people.

# 21 Gossip: newspaper and magazine articles

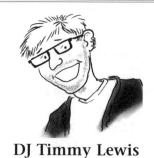

### DJ Timmy Lewis

## Gilli and Timmy's evening in
### (until three o'clock in the morning)

*Another exclusive for CHEERS magazine by our Show Business correspondent Sid Todd*

Spotted yesterday leaving the plush Mayfair home of star DJ Timmy Lewis was none other than Gilli Lollipop. Gilli has been linked with a number of men since she split with all-girl group *The Beautiful People* last year. First there was American rock legend Rick Plutz, but it is believed that Rick is now happily back at the Plutz family home in Malibu. Then Gilli was seen swimming in Jamaica with Peter Bean, nightclub owner of *Beans*. But Gilli has always insisted that she and Timmy Lewis were 'just good friends'. (Oh no, not that one again, Gilli, please!!) Meanwhile, multi-millionaire Timmy, who owns his own record production company as well as the radio station Radio Live, has recently been spotted at *Beans* dating sixteen-year-old model Bronco McGuire, the daughter of sixties drummer Jumbo McGuire of the group *Plastic Underground*. Later a spokesman for Timmy said, 'It's early days, please give them time.'

# Too good to be true?

Yesterday's report in *CHEERS* magazine that now solo singer Gilli Lollipop was seen leaving the house of DJ Timmy Lewis in the early hours, comes just two days before the release of Gilli's second solo record, *It's All For Me*, after her split with *The Beautiful People*. Is the timing too good to be true, or

### Gilli Lollipop

what? The record is thought to be vital for Gilli's solo career after her first release as a solo artist *I Just Wanna Be in Love* did not exactly set the world on fire. Gilli, whose work for Stop Cancer Now was reported in the *Daily News* yesterday, said, 'It's early days, please give Timmy and me time.'

First reading. Choose the best summary of the two texts, a or b.

a  *CHEERS* magazine reported that Gilli Lollipop and Timmy Lewis were girlfriend and boyfriend but the next day the *Daily News* said that Gilli wanted publicity for her new record and so the story was not true.

b  *CHEERS* magazine found out that Gilli Lollipop and Timmy Lewis were boyfriend and girlfriend. The *Daily News* said that was true and they said that Gilli also had a new record coming out soon and that she did a lot of work for organizations like Stop Cancer Now.

Second reading. In a–h which of the two events happened first? Write 1 next to the event which happened first and 2 next to the event which happened second.

a  Peter Bean was Gilli's boyfriend. _____
Rick Plutz was Gilli's boyfriend. _____

b  There was a story in *CHEERS* magazine about Gilli and Timmy. _____
There was a story in the *Daily News* about Gilli and Timmy. _____

c  Timmy was with Gilli until three in the morning. _____
Timmy dated Bronco McGuire. _____

d  Gilli was in a group called *The Beautiful People*. _____
Jumbo McGuire was in a group called *Plastic Underground*. _____

e  Rick Plutz dated Gilli Lollipop. _____
Rick Plutz was in the family home in Malibu. _____

f  Gilli Lollipop made *I Just Wanna Be in Love*. _____
Gilli Lollipop made *It's All for Me*. _____

g  The *Daily News* wrote about the report in *CHEERS* magazine. _____
The *Daily News* wrote about Gilli Lollipop's work for Stop Cancer Now. _____

h  Gilli left the all-girl group *The Beautiful People*. _____
Gilli made a record called *I Just Wanna Be in Love*. _____

# 22 Biography

## *William Shakespeare (1564–1616)*

William Shakespeare was born in Stratford-upon-Avon in 1564. His mother was called Mary Arden. She came from a rich family. His father, John, was a businessman who sold gloves, wool and meat. William went to Stratford Grammar School where he learned a little Latin and Greek. He married Anne Hathaway in 1582. She was eight years older than him. They had three children, Susannah, born in 1583, and the twins Judith and Hamnet, born in 1585. There are no descendants of the Shakespeare family alive today.

It is possible that in 1587 William Shakespeare joined a group of travelling actors and left Stratford because he was in trouble for stealing a deer but nobody is sure if this is true or if the date is correct.

By 1592 he was definitely an actor and playwright in London. In 1599 the Globe Theatre opened in London and most of his 36 or 37 plays were performed there. Nobody is sure exactly how many plays Shakespeare wrote.

The Globe was made of wood. It was round. There was no roof, so if it rained the audience and the actors got wet. The audience stood on three sides of the stage. They were not quiet, as theatre audiences are today. They made a lot of noise, and sometimes they had sword fights. They also ate oranges because of the bad smell everywhere.

Shakespeare wrote three kinds of play: comedies, tragedies and histories. The comedies had happy endings, the tragedies had sad endings (like *Hamlet*) and the histories told the story of the past, either in England (like *Henry V*) or in ancient Rome (like *Julius Caesar*).

Although there were other successful playwrights at the time – especially Christopher Marlowe – Shakespeare was recognized in his own lifetime as one of the finest playwrights of his time. By 1597 he was rich enough to buy New Place, the finest house in Stratford.

In 1613 the Globe burned down during a performance of Shakespeare's *Henry VIII*. The following year Shakespeare retired and went back to New Place in Stratford. In 1616 he died of a fever and he is buried in Holy Trinity Church, Stratford.

In his will he left his wife his second-best bed. This may mean that he did not love his wife very much but it may also mean that he was trying to avoid paying death duties.

First reading. Are these events in Shakespeare's life definite (write D) or possible (write P)?

1  Shakespeare was born in Stratford-upon-Avon. _____

2  Shakespeare stole a deer in Stratford. _____

3  Shakespeare left Stratford in 1587. _____

4  By 1592 Shakespeare was writing plays in London. _____

5  Shakespeare wrote 36 plays. _____

6  Shakespeare wrote three kinds of play. _____

7  Shakespeare was recognized as one of the finest playwrights of his time during his life. _____

8  Shakespeare bought New Place in 1597. _____

9  Shakespeare died in 1616. _____

10  Shakespeare left his wife his second-best bed because he did not want to pay death duties. _____

Second reading. Complete the timeline of Shakespeare's life by writing the date under each event.

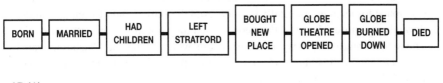

| BORN | MARRIED | HAD CHILDREN | LEFT STRATFORD | BOUGHT NEW PLACE | GLOBE THEATRE OPENED | GLOBE BURNED DOWN | DIED |

*1564* _____ _____ _____ _____ _____ _____ _____

The usual preposition for dates when something actually happened during that month or year is *in* e.g. Shakespeare died *in* 1616. The preposition *by* with a date means that something had been done at some point before this time.

# 23 Novel 1: describing cultures

This is an extract from *The Last Cowboy* by Duane Gerrard.

I was a kid when they built the cattle station in Abilene, though I thought I was a man. It was 1867. I was fifteen and I had loved my first woman and killed my first man. By then we had already killed all the buffalo in Texas and Oklahoma and Kansas. We rode the Chisholm Trail like kings. I was Larry Cabe, the king. How about that?

Then cowboys like us brought cattle in instead of the buffalo. We drove them from Texas along the Chisholm Trail, through Oklahoma all the way to the railroad at Abilene. Every year hundreds of cowboys made that journey.

The Cherokee in Oklahoma were my friends. I used to ride away for the day and meet with Red Hand, son of the Cherokee chief. We hunted all day. That was before the drink got him, like it got so many of his people. Back then they said that the Cherokee drank to live and drank to die. Either way it was a terrible sight to see.

When the first settlers started up their farms in Oklahoma, they were our friends. They were lonely there, on their small farms. They gave us food when we drove the cattle through. Sometimes we stopped and helped them put up the fences around their farms. One settler, Jim Sutter, even wanted me to stay. "We got plenty o' space here," he said to me. "I could use some help. In return, you get half the farm. What d'ya say?" Jim knew I had eyes for Molly, his wife's sister. But I said no. I've never stayed, always moved on.

Then, year after year, there were more farms. And more. There was less and less space for us to get the cattle through. And the settlers didn't want us coming through any more. They lost their cows when they got mixed up with our cattle. The settlers started to carry guns. And somewhere along the Chisholm Trail I started to get old. Twenty years after they built the cattle depot, my teeth and hair were falling out. I felt like an old man.

Then, that last time, there was no way through. The fence at Sutter's farm joined the fences of all the other farms. Jim Sutter stood behind his fence with a rifle. "Let us through, Jim," I said. Behind me two hundred cattle were pawing the ground and the few cowboys I could get by then didn't know what to do with them.

"Jim, I have to get these cattle to Abilene."

"Sorry, Larry. We lost too many cows last year. You can't come through."

My cowboys came up behind me. One of them drew a gun. I said, "Put that away," but even as I spoke Cherokees came out of nowhere. I recognized Red Hand's son, Pale Cloud. I had played with him when he was a kid. Now he wasn't a kid any more and he had a rifle. His shot was the last thing I remember on that long, final ride along the Chisholm Trail.

First reading. Put the events (a–e) in the order that they happened.

| a | There were more and more farms on the Chisholm Trail. | _____ |
| b | Larry Cabe was friends with the Cherokee and the settlers. | _____ |
| c | Red Hand's son, Pale Cloud, shot Larry Cabe. | _____ |
| d | The cattle depot was built in Abilene. | _____ |
| e | Larry couldn't get the cattle through because the fences from all the farms were joined up. | _____ |

Second reading. In each paragraph from the story there are three extra words. Find them and put a line through them.

1   I was a kid when they built the cattle station depot in Abilene, though I thought I was a man. It was 1867. I was fifteen and I had loved my first woman and killed my first man. By then we had already killed some all the buffalo in Texas and Oklahoma and Kansas. We rode the Chisholm Trail like kings. I was Larry Cabe, the king. How think about that?

2   The Cherokee in Oklahoma were never my friends. I used to ride away for the day and meet with Red Hand, son of one the Cherokee chief. We hunted all day. That was before the drink got him, like it got so many of his people. Back then they said that the Cherokee drank to live and drank to die. Either way it was not a terrible sight to see.

3   My cowboys came up with behind me. One of them drew a gun. I said, "Put that away," but even as I spoke cowboys Cherokees came out of nowhere. I recognized Red Hand's son, Pale Cloud. I had played with him when he I was a kid. Now he wasn't a kid any more and he had a rifle. His shot was the last thing I remember on that long, final ride along the Chisholm Trail.

**Background to the story**

Before white men came to America, Native Americans like the Cherokee killed buffalo for food and clothes. The white men killed the buffalo and brought in cattle (cows). From 1867 to the late 1880s cowboys took the cattle to the train station at Abilene (Kansas). But settlers (farmers) started farms with fences round them and the cattle couldn't get through.

# 24 Novel 2: describing a way of life

This is an extract from *Breaking Rules* by Cindy McArthur.

Today is the first day of the rest of your life, right? Right. So why doesn't *somebody* do something about it?

My name is Rhoda Perkins and I live in an old brownstone in Brooklyn with three other girls. I work at JFK airport, at the perfume counter. You fly from JFK and buy perfume, you get me. I'll tell you just one more thing about me. My life sucks.

*10 o'clock July 25:* I should have been at work an hour and a half ago. I phoned the boss.

"Mr. Stevens? Will you go out to dinner with me tonight? … What do you mean, 'why'? Will you or won't you? It's a simple question … No, I'm not coming to work. Forget about work. Will you or won't you go out?"

He hung up.

I got up and dressed to kill. I looked fantastic. I knocked on Annie Kowalsky's door. She has the apartment downstairs. Annie got out of bed, something she does not do as often as most people. "Annie Kowalsky," I said, aiming at the one eye she managed to get open. "You could take the garbage down, maybe once a year?" Kowalsky went into shock and worked on opening the other eye.

"This," I continued, "would be a hundred per cent improvement on your previous record of helping in this house. It would make you a better person. Goodbye."

*11 o'clock:* I walked to *The Dragon Pearl* and had the "Special Feast for Four Persons" for $50, washed down with two pots of jasmine tea. There was nobody else in the place.

*11:45:* Took the subway to Times Square. "This subway station is a disgrace," I told the guy who was sweeping the platform. "Mayor Guiliani has an eight-year plan to clean it up. How can it take eight years to clean up a subway station?"

The cleaning guy smiled. "Don't ask me, lady. I just sweep the floor. Have a nice day."

I took the shuttle to Grand Central Terminal. I was feeling kind of full after the six courses of the "Special Feast for Four Persons". I should maybe have passed up the Peking Duck for, say, three of the persons.

*1:00:* I stopped a cute guy walking his dog outside Grand Central and asked him for a date.

Three months later we got married. Annie Kowalsky was a bridesmaid. I asked Mr. Stevens but he didn't show. Some people have no sense of humor.

First reading. The novel is called *Breaking Rules*. Tick (✓) all the things that Rhoda Perkins did that *you think* break the rules of everyday life.

| | | |
|---|---|---|
| 1 | Rhoda phoned her boss when she didn't get to work on time. | ☐ |
| 2 | Rhoda asked her boss to have dinner when she had not come into work. | ☐ |
| 3 | Rhoda asked Annie Kowalsky to take the garbage down. | ☐ |
| 4 | Rhoda told Annie Kowalsky that taking the garbage down would make her a better person. | ☐ |
| 5 | Rhoda had a six course Chinese meal for four people at 11 o'clock in the morning. | ☐ |
| 6 | Rhoda complained about the mayor's plan to clean up Times Square subway station to one of the cleaners. | ☐ |
| 7 | Rhoda stopped a stranger outside Grand Central Station and asked him for a date. | ☐ |

Second reading. Match the names (1–7) with who or what they are (a–g).

| | | | | |
|---|---|---|---|---|
| 1 | a brownstone | a | mayor of New York at the time of the story |
| 2 | JFK | b | a Chinese restaurant |
| 3 | Mr. Stevens | c | Rhoda's boss |
| 4 | Annie Kowalsky | d | an area of New York |
| 5 | *The Dragon Pearl* | e | a type of house |
| 6 | Mayor Guiliani | f | someone who lives in the same building as Rhoda |
| 7 | Brooklyn | g | an airport in New York City |

> **brownstone** = type of house made of a reddish-brown stone, found in New York City.
>
> **sucks** (American English slang) = is not satisfactory
>
> **garbage** = British English rubbish
>
> **subway** = British English underground or tube
>
> **Peking Duck** = a Chinese dish

# 25 Postcard

Dear Dave,

Well, this is my first time in New Zealand,
but I sure hope it won't be the (1) _____ .
Laura and I are (2) _____ at Waitemata
Harbour, which is relatively busy – though
Auckland only has just over one (3) _____
people. But the beach is one way and the
farms are the other (4) _____ and both are
glorious and there's nobody there! And as
the picture on this (5) _____ shows, for
someone who likes sailing, like you do, this
(6) _____ is paradise. They call it 'the city
of sails'. Maybe one day you and I will visit
Auckland (7) _____ and you can take me
sailing. I'd like that... Speak to you when I
get (8) _____ .

Love, Helen

Dave Smith
10 Wall Road
Newcastle
England

First reading. Write the missing words in the correct place on the postcard.

| back | card | city | last | million | staying | together | way |
|------|------|------|------|---------|---------|----------|-----|

Second reading. True or false?

1    Helen has been to New Zealand before. _____

2    Helen is visiting New Zealand alone. _____

3    Helen has visited the beach and the farms. _____

4    There are more people where Helen is staying than on the beach or at the farms. _____

5    Helen tells Dave she has been sailing. _____

6    Dave likes sailing. _____

7    Helen wants to go back to Auckland one day with Dave. _____

# 26 Youth hostel and hotel information

---

## The Lake District Youth Hostels

The beauty of the Lake District, England's largest National Park, tempts visitors whatever the weather or time of year. Walk or climb in the breathtaking scenery which inspired the poets Wordsworth and Coleridge. Try watersports on Windermere or Coniston Water, or simply wander round the picturesque villages and market towns.

You can explore the area using the Youth Hostel Association's shuttle bus, a door-to-door service that carries you and your backpack to some of the best parts of the Lake District.

With free pick-up from Windermere Railway Station, the shuttle bus takes care of you from the moment you arrive! For more information on this and booking hostels in the Lake District, contact Ambleforth Youth Hostel on 01594 32304.

---

## Lakeside Cabins  Creffield, Lancashire LA5 2JZ

Just half an hour's drive from the glorious scenery of the Lake District, and close to the superb beaches of Morecambe Bay ...

Guests are accommodated in spacious wood cabins around a large lake. Each cabin is beautifully furnished and well equipped for a self-catering holiday. Each has its own luxurious sitting room with satellite television and a well equipped kitchen. The bedroom has an en-suite bathroom.

The resort has a private health and leisure complex with heated pool, gymnasium, steam room and sunbed. And after your swim you can enjoy a drink in the bar in the spacious residents' lounge, or an excellent dinner in the modern restaurant.

Whether you like waterskiing or canoeing, or whether you'd rather sit at the water's edge and feed the ducks, you'll love this resort. And if you've come by car and you want to go sightseeing, you couldn't be better placed.

---

Descriptive language

*breathtaking, glorious, superb, first-class* = very good

*spacious* = big

*luxurious* = very comfortable

*cabin* = small building in the country made of wood that you can sleep in

Note the use of the imperative: *Walk ..., Climb ..., Try ...* In descriptive language, this is an invitation to do these things.

Note also the use of *you* meaning anybody who is on holiday: *You'll love ..., You couldn't be better placed ...*

First reading. Read the text and tick (✓) the grid.

|  | Lake District Youth Hostels | Lakeside Cabins |
|---|---|---|
| 1 watersports |  |  |
| 2 sightseeing |  |  |
| 3 near a lake |  |  |
| 4 not in the Lake District |  |  |
| 5 lots of facilities |  |  |
| 6 not far from the sea |  |  |
| 7 set in beautiful scenery |  |  |

Second reading. Choose the best completion of the sentences, a or b.

1 Visitors go to the Lake District

a) in good weather   b) in good and bad weather

2 Wordsworth and Coleridge

a) owned some of the Lake District
b) wrote poems about the Lake District

3 The shuttle bus connects

a) youth hostels in the Lake District
b) railway stations in the Lake District

4 Phone Ambleforth Youth Hostel to book holidays

a) at Ambleforth   b) in the Lake District

5 At Lakeside Cabins you

a) have to cook all your own food   b) can cook all your own food

6 Each cabin is

a) the same   b) different

7 You can walk from your cabin to

a) the lake   b) the Lake District

# 27 Directions

Read Ed's note to Mark. Choose the correct map or picture, a or b.

Hi Mark,

Looking forward to seeing you on Friday. My new house is easy to find. Take the M28 ring road, heading north. Exit Junction 4 signposted Dimchurch. Continue along the dual carriageway to the roundabout, then take the third exit off the roundabout. About a kilometre along this road you'll see a petrol station on the right and the Hospital Arms pub on the left. Take the next right and that will take you into Dimchurch. Latimer Road is the first on the left after the supermarket. I'm at number 43. You can't miss it!

Cheers!

Ed

**1** a)          b)

**2** a)          b)

**3** a)          b)

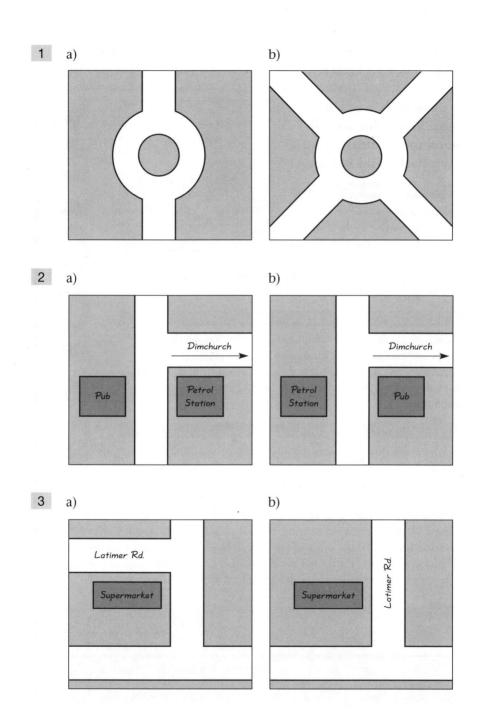

# 28 Holiday brochure

First reading. In the following text there are twelve unnecessary words. Find them and put a line through them.

## A friendly welcome, excellent value and all-round top destination for a fun-packed ski holiday.

France

Andorra

Spain

### The country

Andorra is the an independent principality nestled in the Eastern Pyrenees between countries France and Spain, just 450 kilometres square, but packed with superb skiing, low-priced shopping and lively boring nightlife.

### The best ski schools

The ski schools in Andorra are not known to be among the best in Europe and excellent value for money. The vast majority of instructors don't speak English as their first language and all don't have international British Association of Ski Instructors teaching qualifications.

### Snowboarding

Andorra is fast slow becoming the new European snowboarding mecca.

### Duty-free shopping

If you've skied in other areas of Europe you'll be aware of the high low prices charged for goods and services in the main resorts. Not so in Andorra – its duty-free status means that the prices are unbelievably low, so you can have a good time without spending too much. For the best choice, head for the a capital Andorra la Vella – it's a shopper's paradise with streets lined with bargains.

## ANDORRA FACTS

**DUTY-FREE CURRENCY COUNTRY**
**SIZE:** 468 sq km/65,000 inhabitants
**LANGUAGE:** Catalan, although sometimes French, Spanish and English are widely spoken.
**CURRENCY:** Spanish pesetas or French francs although pesetas are more widely often used.

Second reading. Tick (✓) all the phrases that are about money.

1   a friendly welcome ☐

2   excellent value ☐

3   a fun-packed ski holiday ☐

4   in the Eastern Pyrenees ☐

5   low-priced shopping ☐

6   lively nightlife ☐

7   among the best in Europe ☐

8   excellent value for money ☐

9   teaching qualifications ☐

10  the new European snowboarding mecca ☐

11  high prices charged for goods and services ☐

12  Duty-free status ☐

13  you can have a good time without spending too much ☐

14  head for the capital ☐

15  it's a shopper's paradise ☐

16  streets lined with bargains ☐

*excellent, top, best, unbelievably* = very good

*duty free* = no tax on anything that tourists buy, so things are cheaper.

*mecca* = Here, it means the place everybody goes to.

# 29 Formal letter 1: booking a holiday

Hiroyuki Mahita
Manager
Hotel Sayuri
Bukkoji-dori
Kyoto
Japan

54 Wates Road
Neasden
London
NO6 4RL

16 September 2001

Dear Mr Mahita,

I was given your name and the address of your hotel by two friends of ours who stayed at the *Sayuri* last June. They were Mr James Collins and Mr Arthur Drake. You would perhaps remember James Collins, as he speaks fluent Japanese.

Both Mr Collins and Mr Drake spoke very highly of your hotel and all the help they received from your staff when they visited Kyoto.

Following their recommendation, I would like to make a reservation at your hotel for myself and my friend, Mr Peter Sullivan. We would like two single rooms as close to each other as possible, adjoining would be ideal. We would like to be in Japan for New Year's Day and to be there for Adult's Day (*Seijin-no hi*), which we have been told is on the second Monday in January. So we would like our reservations to be from 31 December 2001 to 20 January 2002.

I have also been told that you can arrange an English-speaking guide, certainly for the *Machiya*, the town houses of Kyoto, but also for other aspects of life in Kyoto. Can you also advise me on car hire in Japan, please?

I look forward to hearing from you with confirmation of the booking and advice on prices and payment – how much do you want in advance as a deposit?

I should perhaps mention that unlike our friend Mr Collins, neither myself nor Mr Sullivan has a single word of Japanese (unfortunately!). But I am told that you speak excellent English.

I look forward to hearing from you.

Yours sincerely,

*T. R. Latham*

Ted Latham

First reading. Tick (✓) all the things that Ted Latham wants Mr Mahita to do.

| | | |
|---|---|---|
| 1 | speak Japanese to James Collins | ☐ |
| 2 | reserve two rooms | ☐ |
| 3 | arrange a guide to the town houses of Kyoto | ☐ |
| 4 | arrange a guide to Kyoto | ☐ |
| 5 | arrange a guide for aspects of life outside Kyoto | ☐ |
| 6 | book a car in Japan | ☐ |
| 7 | find information about booking a car in Kyoto | ☐ |
| 8 | confirm the booking | ☐ |
| 9 | tell him about prices in Japan | ☐ |
| 10 | tell him how much money to send as a deposit | ☐ |
| 11 | reply in English | ☐ |

Second reading. True or false?

1   James Collins liked the *Sayuri* more than Arthur Drake. _____

2   Ted Latham wants a double room. _____

3   Ted Latham wants a room next to Peter Sullivan. _____

4   If a room next to Peter Sullivan is not possible, Ted Latham wants
     a room as close to Peter Sullivan as possible. _____

5   Ted Latham wants rooms at the *Sayuri* from New Year's Day until
     Adult's Day. _____

> This is a formal letter. The writer's address is on the right, the name and
> address of the person receiving the letter is on the left. The date is on the left.
> *Yours sincerely* is used to end a letter which begins *Dear Mr/Mrs/Miss/Ms
> Smith*, etc. *Yours faithfully* is used to end a letter which begins *Dear
> Sir/Madam*.
> In US English, *Yours truly* is an alternative to *Yours sincerely*.

# 30 Formal letter 2: complaint and dispute

```
                                    Flat 6B Peabody Buildings
St Kilda Car and Van Hire           Leith
34 Royal Terrace                    ED8 9TP
Edinburgh
ED4 7BW

8 July 2001

Your ref: SAT/PJ Jul

Dear Sir or Madam,

Return of Citroen ZX P189 OAS hired 30 June 2001
```

I was both distressed and angry to receive your letter dated
6 July. I cannot believe that, as you say, you are threatening
to charge us for collecting the car we hired from you, which is
now in London. And you are also threatening to sue us for loss
of earnings on the car while it is in London and until it is
returned.

    Of course the car should have been returned on 5 July. But my
boyfriend and I were mugged in London. We were both hit in the
face and everything we had on us was stolen, including the keys
to the hire car. This happened on 1 July in London and we phoned
your office from the police station and told you. Unfortunately
we did not take the name of the person we spoke to, but it was a
female with a Liverpool accent.

    As we told this person on the phone, the police refused to
break open the hire car for us. They are not allowed to do that.
So I could not get at my handbag or our luggage. We were
penniless in London and my boyfriend needed hospital treatment
for what those thugs did to him. It was only because I know
people in London and I was able to borrow money that we could
get back to Edinburgh at all.

    On the phone we asked you to collect the car for us, drive it
back to Edinburgh and give us back my handbag and all our
luggage. Will you please do this? As I have explained, we have
no way of doing it ourselves. And please write again withdrawing
all your threats. I think my boyfriend and I have been through
enough, don't you?

Yours faithfully,

*Shiona McPhail*

S McPhail

First reading. Put these events in the order that they happened.

1   The police refused to break into the hired car. _____

2   Shiona phoned the car hire company and told them what had happened. _____

3   The car keys were stolen. _____

4   Shiona and her boyfriend received a letter from the car hire company. _____

5   Shiona and her boyfriend hired a car. _____

6   Shiona and her boyfriend returned to Edinburgh without the car.
_____

Second reading. Match the two halves of these sentences.

1   The car hire company is threatening to charge for collecting the car

2   The car hire company is threatening to sue for loss of earnings

3   Shiona and her boyfriend could not get their luggage out of the car

4   Shiona and her boyfriend could not return the car on time

5   The letter from the car hire company was a surprise to Shiona

a   because the police refused to break it open.

b   because the keys were stolen when they were mugged.

c   because the car was not returned on time.

d   because she had already told them what had happened.

e   because it is not earning any money from the car while it is in London.

This is a very formal letter. The writer has quoted the reference that the firm used (ref:) to file the letter. She also states the subject of the letter under the heading *Dear Sir or Madam*. The letter to her had the same subject.

# 31 Official notes

---

## Application to visit Australia

*Before you apply*
- You must have a passport which is valid for your period of stay in Australia.

- You should carefully read the Conditions for a visitor to Australia below.

*Conditions for a visitor to Australia*
- You must NOT undertake employment while in Australia. A business visitor may only carry out business agreed to by the Australian Government Office.

- You must NOT undertake formal study while in Australia. You may undertake non-formal study – short-term courses of up to three months which are recreational and not subsidized by any government.

**You must leave Australia by the end of the authorized stay.**

*Health insurance*
If your travel insurance does not cover health insurance during your visit, we recommend that you take out private health insurance before your departure. Medical treatment in Australia can be very expensive.

---

Modal *must*, especially *You must NOT*, is only used in official regulations and notes like this. It is very strong!

All these people entered Australia on a visitor's visa from 1 January to 1 March. Tick (✓) if everything is OK and put a cross (✗) if there is a problem.

1   Brian's passport ran out on 2 March. ☐

2   Tracey got a job in a bar. ☐

3   Leslie's business visa allowed her to sell mirrors to Australian hotels. She sold some mirrors and stayed at the hotels. ☐

4   Peter got some money from the US government to learn Japanese for a month. ☐

5   Siti, from Malaysia, learned English for two months. ☐

6   Graham, from Scotland, taught English for two months. ☐

7   Tom started a three-year course at university. ☐

8   Ed left in the middle of March. ☐

9   Susan has fallen ill and she doesn't have private medical insurance. ☐

# 32 Room

This article is adapted from *Women's World* magazine.

## My favourite room

**Actor and playwright Simon Peters tells us about his favourite room.**

My favourite room is my study, at the end of the house. I call it a study but sometimes it's a kitchen and sometimes it's a bedroom, too. Well, it hasn't got a bed but I fall asleep in the armchairs all the time.

My mother, bless her, was very houseproud. We always had to take our shoes off when we came in the room, in case we made the carpet dirty. We couldn't sit back in the armchairs, in case our hair made *them* dirty. So I have old rugs on the floor. I bought this blue one at Dubai Airport when I was flying back from the Middle East, after doing a play out there. And the armchairs are old leather ones I bought second-hand in junk shops. Comfort comes first, you see.

I have a small microwave oven in the corner and a kettle. I make simple meals and coffee late at night. I'm a bit of a night owl and I do most of my writing in the early hours of the morning. I play music then, too. I live alone, so there's nobody to disturb.

On the table there's my computer.

I'm a bit of a computer fan so I have lots of toys like a scanner, that I don't really need. I don't play computer games, though! Next to the computer there's my CD player, which really is important to me. I play everything from Vivaldi to the Beatles but I do like rock music, played loudly.

All around the walls you can see my past. I'm a hoarder – I never throw anything away. You can see certificates I got when I was at school on the walls. And there are photos from a lot of my plays. There are no pictures of me, though. I don't want to see my ugly face when I'm learning my lines or writing.

And now I'll tell you what *isn't* in my room. Because I think you can learn as much about a person from what is not in his room as from what is there. There is no television. There isn't a television in the house. Enough said! And there are no photographs of other people, except actresses and actors who have been in my plays. There's an old saying, you know: 'He walks farthest who walks alone.'

*Simon Peters was talking to Fiona Gage.*

---

*scanner* = copies documents on to a computer
*a night owl* = someone who is more awake at night

First reading. Which of these drawings is Simon Peters's room?

1 ☐  2 ☐  3 ☐

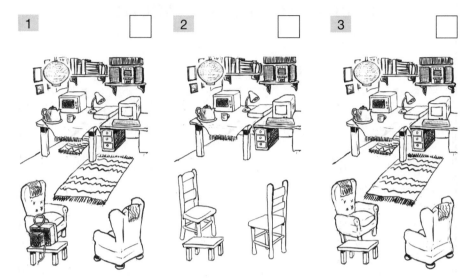

Second reading. Choose the correct answer, a or b?

1   Simon Peters calls his room a study because
a) it is comfortable          b) he works in it

2   He has made the room comfortable because his mother's home
a) was comfortable          b) was not comfortable

3   Everything in the room is
a) old and cheap          b) new and expensive

4   At night Simon Peters
a) sleeps          b) works

5   Simon Peters
a) wants people with him all the time
b) doesn't want people with him very much

# 33 Flat

---

## Brennan's Estate Agent's

Brennan's are delighted to offer this first floor one bedroom flat. To view please call Brennan's on 020 6759 6660.

### PRICE £65,000

LOUNGE: 17'10 x 10'4
KITCHEN: 7'10 x 7'0
BEDROOM: 14'2 x 8'10
BATHROOM/WC

COMMUNAL GARDENS
STORAGE HEATERS
SECURITY ENTRY
LIFT TO ALL FLOORS

*16 Compton Court, Preston, Lancashire*

**The accommodation:**

*ENTRANCE:* Via security entryphone via door into:

*COMMUNAL HALLWAY:* Stairs or lift to own front door.

*HALLWAY:* Storage heater. Cupboard containing water tank. Power points. Door leading to:

*LOUNGE:* 17'10 x 10'4. Double glazed window to front. Storage heater. Security entryphone system. Power point. Telephone point.

*KITCHEN:* 7'10 X 7'0. Wall mounted heater. Wall mounted cupboards. Hob oven and extractor. Stainless steel single sink with mixer tap. Part tiled walls. Space for appliances.

*BEDROOM:* 14'2 x 8'10. Double glazed windows to the front. Storage heater. Fitted wardrobes. Power points.

*BATHROOM/WC* Wall mounted heater. Extractor. WC, hand basin, bath with tiled splashback on the wall.

*EXTERIOR:* There are communal gardens and visitors parking.

---

Choose the best answer to the questions, a, b or c.

In England houses and flats are sold by estate agents (in American English they are called realtors). They have their own special language.

*accommodation or property* = house or flat

*via* = through

*view* = look at

*to* = facing or opposite. For example, *window to front*.

*appliances* = anything you plug in, like fridges or televisions

*communal* = shared

*power points* = places to plug machines in

In Britain, estate agents still use imperial measurements (feet and inches) to give room sizes. One foot (1') = 30.48 centimetres. One inch (1") = 2.54 centimetres. So, 14'2 is about 4 metres 30 centimetres.

1    How many people do you think would live in this flat?

     a) one or two    b) three or four    c) more than four

2    How many floors do you go up in the lift to get to the flat?

     a) one    b) two    c) three

3    What is the biggest room in the flat?

     a) the bedroom    b) the bathroom    c) the lounge

4    Who are the gardens for?

     a) the owner of the flat
     b) the owners of all the flats in the building
     c) the public

5    What helps to keep the flat safe?

     a) the storage cupboard
     b) the telephone point
     c) the entryphone system

6    What helps keep the flat warm?

     a) the storage cupboard
     b) the telephone point
     c) the double glazed windows

7    What can you cook on in the flat?

     a) the integral hob
     b) the extractor
     c) the stainless steel single sink unit

8    What comes out of a mixer tap?

     a) hot water only
     b) cold water only
     c) hot water, cold water or hot and cold water

9    Are there wardrobes in the bedroom now?

     a) yes    b) no    c) we don't know

10    Where is the tiled splashback in the bathroom?

     a) near the bath    b) on the floor    c) on the ceiling

# 34 Novel 3: describing towns

This is an extract from *At the End of the Day* by Stan Sedgwick.

The mine was always the heart of the town. All the men worked down the mine because there was nothing else to do, unless you became a vicar or a professional footballer. And in the last ten years Moxton had had just one of each. Dennis Parker, who was small and very white, had gone down south to be a vicar and Jimmy 'Sniffer' Shaw was the nearest thing Moxton had to a famous son. He played centre forward for Leeds and one game for England. Should have had more.

The mine company ran the Working Men's Club, too. Some of the greatest comedians in the country came to Moxton to tell their jokes at the Working Men's Club. This was the 1930's, radio was around but nobody was very interested. Television hadn't started at all. The comedians toured the country, telling the same jokes over and over again. Nobody had heard them before because nobody went anywhere, outside their own home town. People lived and died in Moxton without ever visiting Featherbridge and that's the village five miles away.

People always ate the same things every day of the week in those days, too. Friday was always fish. There was always beef for Sunday dinner. That is of course if somebody was working to provide the money. No money and it was greens every day, if you were lucky. As late as World War II there were kids in the town who couldn't walk properly because they didn't get any vitamins. Rickets they called it. You could see little kids limping down the town's main street with rickets.

The main street was about all there was of Moxton, too. The houses on either side of it were one line of tiny cottages, all covered in black from the mine. When you walked in you were right in the main room. There was no hall or anything. There was a tin bath in the main room where the miner father washed himself in the evening, after his wife had heated up the water and carried it in.

Sunday was different, of course. Sunday was church and then maybe a walk on the moors. The countryside outside Moxton was green and hilly but somehow people never walked far. They were too tired. The men were old at forty and the women got old even quicker.

---

*mine* = place where miners dig for coal (which is black and was used for heating)

*Leeds* = city in the north of England

*greens* = vegetables like cabbage

*rickets* = disease caused by lack of vitamins, especially vitamin C

*moors* = beautiful green scenery but with few trees

First reading. Answer these questions with one word.

1   How many men from Moxton did not become
    miners?                                              _____

2   Which sport did Jimmy Shaw play?                     _____

3   Was there radio in the 1930s?                        _____

4   The houses in Moxton did not have a hall.
    What other room did they not have?                   _____

5   What did the miners do in the main room
    of their houses?                                     _____

6   What did people do after church on Sunday?           _____

Second reading. Complete the table with words from the text.

| work | food | houses | c _ _ _ _ _ _ _ _ _ |
|------|------|--------|---------------------|
| m _ _ _ _ | g _ _ _ _ _ | c _ _ _ _ _ _ _ | moors |
| c _ _ _ _ _ _ _ | b _ _ _ | | |
| v _ _ _ _ | fish | | |
| p _ _ _ _ _ _ _ _ _ _ | footballer | | |

# 35 Autobiography: describing scenery

This is an extract from *If I Can Make It Anybody Can* by Victoria Rothesay.

After I left Debrecen I walked for days and put up my tent at night. An old couple driving a horse and cart stopped and spoke to me. I tried out my broken Hungarian and they laughed. But it was obvious they were offering me a lift, so I got up on the cart, with my backpack and tent. They offered me some fiery apricot liqueur, home-made by the look of it. We drank it from the bottle.

The land was flat. You could see forever. You could see as far as the future. At first we could still see the Hortobagy River, brown in the weak sunshine, and carpets of sunflowers. But then, as we jolted along a track in the cart, there was just the *puszta* – the dry Great Plain of Hungary. It's where the Hungarians grow their wheat and catch their wild horses.

A Hungarian poet once said that the earth and the sky are one in the *puszta*. I understand what he means. As far as you can see in every direction, the sky comes down and touches the land. This dry yellow land is not beautiful in the usual sense, but being in it, being part of it, I felt a great sense of peace. I have always hated mountains and skyscrapers because they are bigger than I am. But this ... When I lay down and watched the *puszta* from the back of the cart, it was like being in a great safe flat bed that had no sides but just went on forever. It was then, at that moment, that I felt I could do anything in the world that I wanted. I was eighteen years old.

Then, in the distance, we saw the horses. At first there was just a cloud of dust. Then, suddenly, about ten small, wiry, brown Hungarian wild horses charged across the Great Plain. They got near enough for me to see them tossing their heads. Two *csikos*, Hungarian cowboys, were chasing them. The cowboys saw the cart and shouted something. The old man shouted something back and he and the old woman laughed. They said something to me in Hungarian, probably trying to explain what the cowboys had said.

I fell asleep. When I woke up, the horses and the two *csikos* had gone but nothing about the scenery had changed. We were still moving forward but it was as if we had stopped.

I didn't want us ever to arrive anywhere. I wanted to stay on that cart in the Great Plain forever. But at the same time I knew that when the journey was over, everything was going to be just fine. And it was.

First reading. True or false?

1  Debrecen is a town in Hungary. _____

2  The writer speaks no Hungarian at all. _____

3  The writer saw the Hortobagy River. _____

4  The writer felt a sense of peace because nothing in the scenery was bigger than her. _____

5  The writer likes flat scenery better than mountains. _____

6  The Hungarian cowboys didn't see the cart. _____

7  The scenery on the Great Plain doesn't change very much. _____

8  The writer describes a moment when she knew that everything in her life would be fine. _____

Second reading. Match the describing words and phrases (1–6) with what they describe (a–f).

1  broken

2  fiery

3  carpets

4  weak

5  the sky and the earth are one

6  tossing their heads

a  an alcoholic drink

b  flat scenery

c  horses

d  flowers

e  sunshine

f  the writer's Hungarian

# 36 Advertisements: for sale

**a**

Ford Fiesta N reg
5 Door hatchback
cassette player,
central locking, sunroof
Low mileage.
Full service history.
£2,500 o.n.o
tel: 569832

**b**

Viduka 4 Star Royale Pram
Plum coloured, white tyres, v.g.c
£100 o.n.o
Also baby changing unit
(bought at Mothercare)
£20 or £10 if you buy the pram too.
tel: 863196

**c**

Eptron 776 Computer
WORD 6 and internet access.
Instruction manual but could
give training. Immaculate
condition – owner going abroad
£350
Box: 665

**d**

FREE TO A GOOD HOME
Black Scottie dog aged five.
Loving and house trained.
I am moving and can't take
him with me. v good with children
Box: 776

**e**

Mountain Bike – Drake SJ5
5 gear, new saddle, new tyres.
Bought new 3 years ago.
£150
Also cycle helmet free with
FULL amount.
tel: 245591

**f**

Bride's dress size 12 satin, off-white,
not worn
£150
Also three turquoise bridesmaids dresses,
suit girls between six and nine.
£50 each or £120 the three
Box: 331

Read the advertisements and answer the questions.

**1**  Which advertisement is offering something not used?  _____

**2**  Which advertisements give a reason for selling?  _____

**3**  Which advertisements offer a definite price?  _____

**4**  Which advertisement offers no price?  _____

**5**  Which advertisements offer prices that are different
according to what you buy?  _____

**6**  Which advertisements tell you the colour of what they
are selling?  _____

**7**  Which advertisements tell you something about
the past of what they are selling?  _____

**8**  Which advertisements use complimentary words to
tell you that what they are selling is really good?  _____

**9**  Which advertisement gives you something free
if you buy what they are selling?  _____

*box* = The customer doesn't want to give a telephone number, so the shop
or supermarket where the noticeboard is will collect any enquiries to that
box number and send them on.
*o.n.o* = or nearest offer
*v.g.c* = very good condition
*service history* = a record of the car being serviced at a garage
*baby changing unit* = a stand you put a baby on to change its nappy

# 37 Internet: buying and booking

**DO IT NOW –
JUST FOR FUN**

# justforfun.com

## UK home offers

- cars
- flights
- holidays
- entertainment
- restaurants
- presents
- useful information
- help?
- register now
- about the newsletter
- about justforfun.com guarantees
- security
- jobs with the company

**Who do you love most in the world? Why not give them a justforfun.com gift voucher?**

You said:

*I booked my dream holiday in Rome with justforfun.com. The booking was easy and reps Sylvie and Graham were fantastic. I'm booking with you next year.*

**Do you want to talk? We have real live people here you can talk to online.**

**Just click here.**

**SUBSCRIBE TO THE AMAZING NEWSLETTER. YOU'LL KNOW EVERYTHING ABOUT EVERYTHING.**

**It's free click here.**

| Today's best offers from everything | |
|---|---|
| ① Giants Smash Hit play Under £5 offer (£4.99) | ③ The Funny Boys world tour (£35 2 for the price of 1 including booking fee) |
| ② Top singer Adam Jam in concert £30 | ④ Exclusive party for London Fashion Week (£30) |
| | ⑤ River Trip for Two on London's lovely Thames (£40) |

## Our very best deals from cars

Something new: crossover vehicles like the Energy Sport Car, which is a mix of an electric car and a pick-up truck. What else is new to buy?

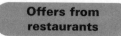
**next step/info/more offers**

## Offers from restaurants

London's top eaterie Mama's Pantry – special deal for justforfun customers

**next step/info/more offers**

## Offers from stargazing

Come to the preview screening of The New Wave on June 10th (opens June 15th). Mix with the stars afterwards

**next step/info/more offers**

## Holidays

Paris for the weekend. Stay at the exclusive Toulouse Lautrec and eat at Gerrards

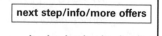
**next step/info/more offers**

▶ ▶ ▶ ▶ ▶ ▶

Choose the correct answers. *Sometimes there is more than one correct answer.*

1   You are on the justforfun.com website and you have a problem. Click on

a) register now     b)  help?     c)  Do you want to talk?

2   You are worried about buying on the Internet. Click on

a) guarantees     b) security     c) jobs with the company

3   You want a nice evening with your partner but you have only £15 to spend. Click on

a) River trip for two     b) London's top eaterie
c) *Giants* Smash Hit play

4   You want a weekend holiday. Click on

a) Paris for the weekend     b) UK home offers holidays
c) You said I booked my dream holiday

5   You want to book a restaurant in London but you went to Mama's Pantry last week. Click on

a) Mama's Pantry next step     b) Mama's Pantry info
c) Mama's Pantry more offers

6   You think you will visit the justforfun.com website often. You should visit

a) subscribe to the newsletter     b) register now
c) jobs with the company

7   You want an ordinary car. You should visit

a) UK home offers cars     b) from cars Energy Sport Car next step
c) UK home offers presents

Internet language
***click on*** = gives you more information
Sometimes a bullet point • can give you more information too.

# 38 Products: mail order

## Buy 3-piece luggage set for only £69.99
### Half price offer

*Pack with confidence, Travel in Style ... Arrive Intact*
*This elegant luggage is manufactured in a new hard-wearing plastic*
*which is strong and very light in weight.*

- Light but hard-wearing
- Strong retractable handles and robust wheels for ease in travel
- 3 locks (2 key and 1 combination lock) for total security
- Supplied with initials for personalization

**MD 9572 £69.99**

ALL ORDERS DELIVERED FREE TO YOUR DOOR

## Plan your journey the easy way

*This handy Traveller will give you directions from A to B anywhere in England, Scotland and Wales. Just enter the start and destination of your journey and the Traveller will work out the quickest route. Specify a route that includes or avoids motorways or goes via certain places. The Traveller can also estimate the journey time, average speed and fuel consumption. Need to alter your journey at any stage? The Traveller will give you a new set of directions. Other features include auto shut-off and a built-in light for night-time use. Powered by 4 AA batteries (not supplied)*

**MD 7437 Traveller £69.99**

## How much do you know?

*Everyone, young and old, enjoys the challenge of quizzes. Our electronic Quizmaster contains 5,400 questions and answers in 6 categories – general knowledge, sport, science, geography, art and history. Each of these is subdivided into 3 skill levels (easy, medium and difficult) so younger children can fairly compete against teenagers and adults. PLUS! Every Quizmaster includes:*

- 8 Games of Hangman
- Anagrams and Fortune Teller Games
- 10-digit calculator/convertor
- long life cell batteries included
  (11 x 6.5 x 1cm)

**MD 9659 Quizmaster was £19.99 now £14.99**

---

Selling language

*handy* = useful

*elegant* = looks good

*includes/supplied with* = comes with

Mail order advertisements often use rhetorical questions (questions that don't need an answer). For example, *Need to alter your journey at any stage?*

Read the mail order advertisements and answer the questions.

**1** Tick (✓) the phrases which give you *factual* information about the luggage in the first advertisement.

a) 3-piece ☐

b) Pack with confidence ☐

c) Arrive in style ☐

d) light in weight ☐

e) retractable handles ☐

f) 3 locks (2 key and 1 combination) ☐

**2** Tick (✓) the four sentences which could be from the *Traveller*.

a) Here are your directions from London, England, to Edinburgh, Scotland. ☐

b) Here are your directions from Ghent, Belgium, to Bruges, Belgium. ☐

c) Here are all the garages along your chosen route. ☐

d) Here is your route from London to Birmingham (England) via Oxford. ☐

e) Here is your route from London to Birmingham (England) with no motorway driving. ☐

f) Here is your route from London to Birmingham (England) using the least fuel. ☐

g) Your journey from London to Birmingham (England) will take two and a half hours at an average speed of 60 mph and you will use 30 litres of petrol. ☐

**3** Are these comments about the *Quizmaster* true or false?

a) You never know the answer when it asks a question. _____

b) You have to buy your own batteries. _____

c) The questions are either easy or difficult, there's nothing between. _____

d) You can't get a question like 'Who was the number 1 men's tennis player in the world at the end of the year 2000?' _____

e) When you have asked 5,400 questions there is nothing else to do. _____

f) It is for adults only. _____

g) There is a calculator with it. _____

# 39 Clothes: mail order

## Boots (men's)

By the Union Team.
Leather with a plastic sole.
Sizes: 3, 4, 5

**Order number:**
**PQ 2544** black
**PQ 2545** dark brown
£29.99 (20 weeks @ £1.49)

## Three-quarter length jacket

(women's)
Fashionable leather.
Fully lined. Length 34 ins.
Do not hand clean.
Sizes: 10, 12, 14, 16, 18

**Order number:**
**CQ 8200** black
**CQ 8201** black
£99.99 (40 weeks @ £2.49)

**INSURE YOUR LEATHER JACKET**
**against theft and accidental damage.**
**For details see page 1143**

## Swimsuit (women's)

By Swimglam.
In soft fabric for high comfort.
Made of:
80% micropolyamide
20% elastane.
Sizes: 10, 12, 14, 16

**Order number:**
**GQ 9292** navy/turquoise
£19.99 (20 weeks @ 99p)

## The MAGIC jeanswear collection (women's)

Stretch denim in 4 colours and three lengths.
Made to sit slightly lower than natural
waistline at front. Zip fastening. Washable.
Made of: 96% cotton 4% elastane.
Sizes: 10, 12, 14, 16

**Order number:**
**GQ 8487** dark blue
**GQ 8488** black
£24.99 (20 weeks @ £1.24)

## Epaulette shirt (men's)

Short-sleeved shirt with sleeve and shoulder
epaulettes, button-down collar and two
button-down chest pockets. Washable.
Cotton.
Sizes: S (35/37), M (38/40), L (41/43), XL (44/46)

**Order number:**
**KQ 8149** beige
**KQ 8151** dark green
£14.99 (20 weeks @ 74p)

## Classic rugby shirts (men's)

In the same style as your rugby team –
Scotland, England or Wales.
All our stylish rugby shirts are genuine
leisure shirts too. They're all machine
washable and in 100% cotton.
Sizes: S, M, L, XL

**Order number:**
Scotland shirt: **KQ 9967**
England shirt: **KQ 9963**
Wales shirt: **KQ 9979**
£19.99 (20 weeks @ 99p)

Sizes are different in England from other countries in Europe and the USA.
Sizes are often still given in inches in catalogues.

*S* = small, *M* = medium, *L* = large, *X* or *XL* = very large.

Catalogue goods always have an order number, which you use when you buy.

First reading. True or false?

1   The sole of the men's boots is made of leather. _____

2   You can get the men's boots in two colours. _____

3   The leather jacket is already insured when you buy it. _____

4   It is cheaper to pay for the leather jacket over forty weeks. _____

5   You can get the swimsuit in black. _____

6   The swimsuit comes in four sizes. _____

7   The jeans have a zip. _____

8   You wear the jeans low. _____

9   XL is the biggest size you can get the epaulette shirt in. _____

10   The order number for a green epaulette shirt is KQ 81 49. _____

11   The rugby shirt is for playing rugby and wearing with (for example) jeans. _____

12   The rugby shirt is like the shirt worn by the rugby teams. _____

Second reading. Tick (✓) the phrases which give you information, not opinions, about the product.

1   fashionable

2   Do not hand clean

3   20% elastane

4   washable

5   with sleeve and shoulder epaulettes

6   stylish

# 40 Offers

**A**

### We'll refund 3X the difference

With our new **PRICE WATCH** promise on selected items we aim to offer the best possible prices. If you find the same product locally at a cheaper price, we promise to refund three times the difference. We're the only store to do so – from your nearest superstore to your local late shop. So why search far and wide for the best deals? Just look for the **PRICE WATCH** sign at participating stores:
**JMB STORES**

**B**

**A great offer for new E&F customers**

*This voucher entitles you to 10% off a complete pair of glasses (frames and lenses) from Edelhoff and Farouk on or before 10 May.*

At Edelhoff and Farouk we help you find the perfect glasses. When you visit our local store you are entitled to our free style and colour consultation service – Facefit. Our expert staff will help you select frames that suit your face shape, skin tone and lifestyle.

**C**

### BOOKS-R-US
### *first in paperbacks*

Any 5 books for only 50p each plus p&p plus an exclusive Books-R-Us wallet FREE
save up to £103
90 books to choose from
*To introduce you to Books-R-Us you can choose any five books for only 50p each (plus a total of £2.95 p&p)*
As a member you get a discount of up to 50% on the retail price of every title.
The single thing we ask is that you buy at least six books during your first year of membership.

**D**

**A FREE GIFT**
from
**SHEER DELIGHT**

*Magnifying up to 8 times to let you see the smallest details, these ADVENTURER's BINOCULARS can be carried everywhere. They will be sent to you absolutely free with your SHEER DELIGHT order.*

**Dear Madam, Dear Sir**

*Summertime is with us and to celebrate SHEER DELIGHT has a whole range of totally new products to present to you.*

**E**

## WANTED
### Your old shoes
### £10 Reward
**Take any old pair of shoes into HILO's Flagship Store in Oxford Street between now and 30 September and you will receive ten pounds off any new pair of fully priced HILO shoes, (one pair per purchase). Your old shoes will go to a Third World country.**

**F**

### Goslings Furniture Summer Sale

Dear Mr Haynes,
As a valued customer, we would like to invite you to our Preview Week commencing 9.15 am Saturday 10th June, before the Sale starts to the General Public.
During this week we would like to offer you:
• up to ten months interest free credit or
• vouchers worth up to £375 extra discount

*p & p* = the cost of postage and packing
*retail price* = the price in a shop

First reading. Read the offers and answer the questions.

1 Which offer or offers do you pay less with? _____

2 Which offer or offers give you something? _____

3 With which offers could you buy more than one type of item? _____

4 With which offer do you change something for something else? _____

5 Which offer is definitely not for new customers? _____

Second reading. Write the word or phrase from the offers that tells you that all these statements are wrong.

Offer A

1 You can get money back with PRICE WATCH at all JMB stores. *participating*

2 You can get money back with PRICE WATCH on any item. _____

3 You can get money back with PRICE WATCH if you find a cheaper price in another country. _____

Offer B

4 You can keep the E & F voucher and use it in ten years' time. _____

Offer C

5 When you join Books-R-Us you pay a total of £2.50 for five books. _____

6 When you are a member of Books-R-Us you are guaranteed to get books for half the price they are in the shops. _____

Offer D

7 You can get a pair of binoculars free when you write to SHEER DELIGHT. _____

Offer E

8 If you have ten pairs of old shoes you can buy ten pairs of new ones and save £100.

_____

9 If you buy shoes in the Sale you pay £10 less than the Sale price. _____

10 You can take your old shoes into HILO at any time and get £10 off a new pair.

_____

Offer F

11 This invitation to Preview Week is for anybody that reads it. _____

12 The General Public can come to Preview Week. _____

13 You can get interest free credit *and* vouchers at Preview Week. _____

# 41 Informal letter 3: describing a computer

This is an extract from a 'round robin' letter sent by Tina Laidlaw to her friends at Christmas.

---

... And now to the Great Tina Computer Saga! You all know me and computers. Do we get on? No, we do not. At work when it freezes I just call the supervisor, shout 'computer problem' and go and have a coffee. BUT in a moment of madness I bought a new computer of my own.

It came through the post and my friend Gloria helped me assemble it. She's wonderful with computers. But then we fell out, so I was on my own. For anybody who's interested, it's a BENCRON 825 (or it was). Really state of the art. It has loudspeakers, video, a modem and a scanner. It has a two-speed colour printer ... It can do everything except make you a cup of tea. But unfortunately it doesn't actually work very well.

Problems started on Day 1. I typed an e-mail saying 'Hello everybody, I've got a new computer,' and then it switched itself off before I could send the e-mail. The simplest things online were a problem. I was just talking to this guy in a Chat Room and it switched itself off again. Start-up was a problem too.

This actually got serious when I tried to work from home one day a week. They sent me attached e-mail files from the office but I couldn't download them.

Anyway, in the end it blew up. Apparently the fan wasn't working and it overheated. I have made friends with Gloria again and in future I'm going to use her computer. And now to other news from the past year ...

---

A 'round robin' letter is the same letter sent to all the writer's acquaintances and friends, often at the end of the year, saying what the writer has been doing.

First reading. Tick (✓) the grid with your answers.

|  | parts of a computer | things a computer does (operations) | problems |
|---|---|---|---|
| 1 it freezes |  |  | ✓ |
| 2 loudspeakers |  |  |  |
| 3 modem |  |  |  |
| 4 it doesn't ... work |  |  |  |
| 5 download files |  |  |  |
| 6 start-up |  |  |  |
| 7 attach a file |  |  |  |
| 8 it blew up |  |  |  |
| 9 the fan |  |  |  |
| 10 a scanner |  |  |  |

Second reading. Match the words (1–5) with the definitions (a–e).

1 freezes     a   keeps the computer cool and stops it overheating

2 modem     b   a file (information) sent with an e-mail

3 download files     c   the computer 'stops' and you have no control over it

4 fan     d   put files into your computer

5 attached file     e   device that lets you get on to the internet or send e-mails

# 42 Informal letter 4: describing clothes

This is an extract from a letter from Laura to Becky. Laura and Becky, aged 16, were very good friends before Becky moved to Australia.

*from me*

Hiya!!

How ya doin' down there in Australia?

I have been SHOPPING!! (Yes!). I got this really nice black dress. It covers the shoulder but it's got bare arms and a satin bow type thing high up. I got it at S&R, you know, in the High Street?

And I got some pedal pushers at Hurricane. They come in a pack of two. I got black and stone. They come just below the knee and they've got this pocket thing, but you can't get anything in it. They are a bit tight round the bum, but they look good (I think, I hope, per - lease!!)

Then there were these vest-type tops for the summer. They come in a pack of two as well. They've got very thin straps. One of them's blue and one's lemon.

Lastly (well I got tired!) I got these sling-back sandals so I can paint my toenails and it, like, shows. (No point doing stuff that doesn't show, say I)

And so to boys. I .....

---

Informal writing, especially by teenagers, comes very close to speech.

*per – lease* = please

*you know* and *like* are both features of speech that you also find in informal writing. They are 'fillers' and don't actually mean anything.

First reading. Write the correct letter under the picture of what Laura bought.

| a | black dress |
|---|---|
| b | pedal pushers |

| c | vest tops |
|---|---|
| d | sling-back sandals |

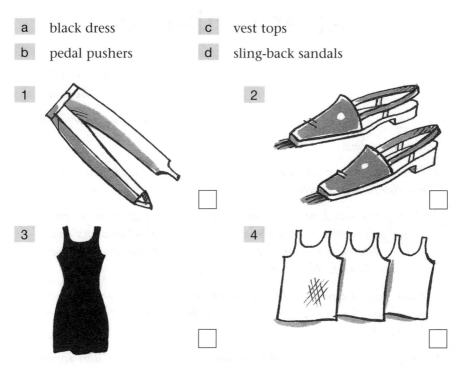

Second reading. Tick (✓) the grid with the correct answer.

|  | black dress | pedal pushers | vest tops | sandals |
|---|---|---|---|---|
| 1 thin straps |  |  |  |  |
| 2 shows the toenails |  |  |  |  |
| 3 blue and lemon |  |  |  |  |
| 4 bought at Hurricane |  |  |  |  |
| 5 pocket |  |  |  |  |
| 6 pack of two |  |  |  |  |
| 7 black and stone |  |  |  |  |
| 8 bought at S&R |  |  |  |  |
| 9 a satin bow |  |  |  |  |

# 43 Informal letter 5: letter of thanks

35 Arthur Way
Swansea

25 November 2001

Dear Grandma,

1 Thank you ever so much for the lovely rucksack you sent for my thirteenth birthday.

2 All my friends have got one but nobody's is as nice as mine! I really love the smiley face on the back. And also it's really roomy. It's now called 'Fred', by the way, after my geography teacher Freddy Frog (that's not his real name).

3 Mum says I can use the rucksack for school as well as when we go to the sea on holiday. I couldn't wait until the summer to use it.

4 I hope you are well and that your leg is better. Mum sends her love.

Lots of love
Kirsty

**1**    Match the subjects (a–d) with the paragraph numbers (1–4) in the letter.

   a    saying how good the present is       _____

   b    saying what the receiver will do with the present       _____

   c    sending good wishes to the giver       _____

   d    thanking the giver for the present       _____

**2**    Which of these do you think made grandma laugh?

   a    Mum says I can use the rucksack for school.

   b    I hope you are well and that your leg is better.

   c    ... Freddy Frog (that's not his real name).

# 44 Rhymes

---

**A**

**THERE WAS AN OLD MAN OF PERU**

There was an old man of Peru,
Who dreamt he was eating his (1) _shoe_.
He woke up in the (2) _____
In a terrible fright,
And found it was perfectly true.

**B**

**I EAT MY PEAS WITH HONEY**

I eat my peas with honey,
I've done it all my life,
It makes the peas taste (3) _____ ,
But it keeps them on the (4) _____ .

**C**

**THERE ONCE WAS A MAN OF BENGAL**

There once was a man of Bengal,
Who was asked to a fancy dress ball
He murmured, 'I'll risk it
and go as a (5) _____ ',
But a dog ate him up in the (6) _____ ,

**D**

**AS I WAS COMING DOWN THE STAIR**

As I was coming down the stair
I met a man who wasn't (7) _____ .
He wasn't there again today;
I *wish* that man would go (8) _____ .

---

First reading. Write the missing words in the rhymes.

> away    biscuit    funny    hall    knife    night    ~~shoe~~    there

Second reading. There are two types of rhyme on this page, *nonsense rhymes* and *limericks*. Answer the questions about them.

**1**   In a *limerick,* lines 1, 2 and 5 rhyme, and lines 3 and 4 rhyme. Which two rhymes are limericks? _____

**2**   In one of the *nonsense rhymes* on this page, lines 1 and 3 rhyme, and lines 2 and 4 rhyme. Which nonsense rhyme is that? _____

**3**   In the other *nonsense rhyme,* lines 1 and 2 rhyme, and lines 3 and 4 rhyme. Which nonsense rhyme is that? _____

*a fancy dress ball* = a formal party where people dress up (go) as somebody else
*nonsense* = something that has no sense – it is very silly

# 45 Cartoon

*Teenage Monster* is a cartoon about a green monster who shares a flat with three girls.

*Country Doc* is a cartoon about a doctor who gets everything wrong.

*Dino* is an American cartoon about a dinosaur.

Read the cartoons and choose the correct sentence completion, a or b.

**About *Teenage Monster***

1    In the cartoon, a job is

    a)   a career like teacher or lawyer.

    b)   something you do to help out in the house.

2    Hoovering is

    a)   cleaning the carpets with a hoover.

    b)   cleaning the windows with a hoover.

3    The joke is that

    a)   the monster wants to help by making a mess.

    b)   the girls want to clean and the monster wants to make everything dirty.

**About *Country Doc***

4    'I'm very sorry' means

    a)   the doctor made a mistake.

    b)   the doctor is unhappy.

5    Mrs Jones says goodbye because

    a)   she thinks her husband is dead.

    b)   she wants to close his eyes.

6    The joke is that Mr Jones

    a)   is not dead and the doctor said he was.

    b)   is dead and the doctor said he wasn't.

**About *Dino***

7    'Dinosaurs got no future' means

    a)   dinosaurs don't think about tomorrow.

    b)   there will be no dinosaurs soon.

8    'Gonna' means

    a)   is going to.

    b)   has gone.

9    The *Dino* cartoon is funny because the reader knows

    a)   the dinosaur is right.

    b)   the dinosaur is wrong.

# 46 Comic

In this comic story, Lauren, Steve and Charlene are Australians in their teens, sharing a flat in Melbourne.

mate = friend. It is common in Australian English, when being friendly.

intense = too serious

creep = a negative, informal word, often used to describe someone people don't like especially someone who is always following you or ringing you when you don't want them to.

First reading. Which summary of the story has no mistakes in it, a or b?

**a** Lauren didn't want to see Paul when he came to the flat. She couldn't go out with him, because she was working at the pizza parlour. At the pizza parlour she didn't speak to Paul. After the pizza parlour closed Paul was angry because she hadn't spoken to him. Lauren was scared of him and she phoned Charlene and told her to come and get her in the car. Steve told everybody to get in the car. Back in the flat Lauren told Charlene that Paul was too intense and she didn't like him any more. In the other room, Paul was crying. Steve told him to go and say sorry to Lauren.

**b** Paul asked Lauren out but she was working at the pizza parlour that evening. Although he had two tickets for the cinema, Paul didn't go but went to the pizza parlour. There he saw Lauren talking to somebody and he got jealous. After Lauren left the pizza parlour he stopped her and asked her out again. Lauren was afraid of him, so she phoned Charlene and told her to bring Steve. Back at the flat Lauren wasn't sure that she had done the right thing when she phoned for help. Meanwhile, Steve told Paul to write to Lauren and not to try and see her again.

Second reading. True or false?

1 Lauren knew Paul was coming when he came to the flat. _____

2 Lauren told Paul that she was working at the pizza parlour that night but that was not true. _____

3 Paul didn't like Lauren talking to someone else at the pizza parlour. _____

4 Paul waited for Lauren to talk to her after work. _____

5 Charlene was angrier with Paul than Steve was. _____

6 Lauren liked Paul but thought he was too intense. _____

7 Paul was crying because of what he had done. _____

8 Steve told Paul to write to Lauren and say he was sorry. _____

# 47 Jokes

Match the questions (1–6) with the answers (a–f) in these jokes.

1 What did one maths books say to the other maths book?

2 What is white and climbs trees?

3 How do you tell when an elephant has been in the fridge?

4 Why do birds fly south for the winter?

5 What do you call a boomerang that doesn't come back?

6 What do you call a scared cow?

a From the footprints in the butter.

b A coward.

c I have problems.

d Because it's too far to walk.

e A fridge. I lied about the climbing.

f A stick.

Match the correct punch lines (a–f) with the jokes (1–6).

**1** There's a white house, a red house and a blue house. The red house is on the left, the blue house is on the right. Where's the White House?

**a** Those who can count and those who can't.

**2** I went to the bank last week and said to the cashier, 'Can you check my balance?'

**b** now I'm perfect.

**c** No, who wrote it?

**3** There are only three kinds of people in the world.

**d** To blame it on the computer is even more natural.

**4** I used to be big-headed but

**e** In Washington DC.

**5** Have you read Shakespeare?

**f** She pushed me over.

**6** It's natural to make mistakes.

Here's one to tell your friends – just for fun!

A dog walked into the Post Office and asked to send a telegram. The counter clerk gave him the form and the dog wrote 'Woof – woof – woof – woof – woof – woof.' The counter clerk looked at the form and said, 'For the same money you could have one more woof.'

'No,' said the dog. 'It wouldn't make sense.'

The punch line of a joke is the line that makes you laugh (hopefully!).
**Noah** = In the Bible, he was a man who set out in the Ark (a kind of boat) with two of every kind of animal in the world. A flood covered the world with water and everyone died apart from the people and animals on the Ark.
**boomerang** = a piece of wood that comes back when you throw it. It is traditionally used by Australian aborigines when they are hunting.

# 48 Adventure story

This is an extract from *How the Boy and I took on the World* by Clancy Gardell.

Jeb Smith was thirty when his wife died. The boy – Skip – was six and he took it bad. The day after the funeral Jeb Smith closed the mountain supplies store he ran in Alamosa. He turned his back on the Rio Grande and he and Skip headed for the San Juan Mountains. They kept to the valleys and gullies, Jeb pushing the boy real hard, lifting him over boulders and rocks when he got tired until they both burned out their pain in the heat.

The cougar saw them before they saw it. It was stretched out in the sun on a ledge of rock, about head high. Jeb saw it as it put its head down between its paws to spring. He put his pack down, quickly. He was wearing a jacket, the way men from the mountains often do, even in the heat, and he pulled the jacket open with both hands, making himself look big to the cougar. It worked. The cougar hesitated, ready to pounce on Jeb, but ready to forget the whole thing, too.

Jeb let go of his jacket, grabbed Skip and held him across his body, making a cross. Now the cougar's enemy looked even bigger and he raised up out of the crouch, ready to slink away, but unfortunately Skip got scared and struggled free of Jeb.

"Skip, no!" yelled his father.

But Skip broke and ran and that's the last thing you do with a cougar. The second Skip broke free, Jeb hurled himself at the cougar, just as it sprang from the rock. They hit each other in mid-air, spun and both fell. The cougar was on Jeb in a flash, forgetting about Skip, which was what Jeb wanted.

Cougars are not as big as most people think and a determined man stands a chance, even with just his fists. As the cougar's claws ripped into his left shoulder, Jeb swiped his fist at its eyes and hit true. The animal howled, hissed and put its head back. Jeb followed up with his other fist, but he only managed to cuff the cougar harmlessly behind the ear. Then out of the corner of his eye, Jeb saw Skip. The boy was running back to help his father.

A low sob broke from Jeb at this but he never stopped swinging his arms, elbows and fists into the cougar's face, so fast that the cougar never got a bite back. But its claws were still digging into Jeb's shoulder and Jeb knew that if he lost consciousness, the cougar would kill both him and Skip.

"Knife, Skip," shouted Jeb.

The boy ran to his father's pack that was lying on the ground and tore at the tent that was folded on top of it. He got the pack open and threw stuff out until he came to the knife. Jeb started yelling as well as hitting, to keep the cougar's attention away from Skip.

Skip got the knife and ran over to Jeb. The cougar was moving its head in and out, trying to find a way through the wall Jeb was making out of his arms. Skip swung with the knife, into the cougar's back. It howled horribly, turned and snarled, and ran off into the mountains.

The whole fight had taken maybe thirty seconds.

First reading. Write *Yes* if you should do these things when you see a cougar and *No* if you should not do them.

1 make yourself look bigger _____

2 make yourself look a funny shape to the mountain lion _____

3 run away _____

4 fight back if it attacks you _____

5 hit the cougar's eyes _____

6 hit the cougar behind the ears _____

Second reading. Match the words with the definitions.

| | | | |
|---|---|---|---|
| 1 | gullies | a | large rocks |
| 2 | boulders | b | jumped |
| 3 | ledge | c | hit gently, on or near the head |
| 4 | sprang | d | very quickly |
| 5 | in a flash | e | like toes on a mountain lion but very sharp |
| 6 | claws | f | when you cry loudly |
| 7 | cuff | g | narrow bed of rock |
| 8 | a sob | h | small, narrow valleys |

# 49 Love story

This is an extract from *Tales of Early Life* by Patricia Field.

L ORRAINE LIKED ART BEST because he sat next to her in art. She liked the sound of his name. She could say it perfectly in her head, Thomas Baldwin. But she couldn't say it out loud at all. The two words of his name got all tangled as they came out, the way so many words do when you are only nine years old.

At least, *she* was nine years old. He was ten. His birthday was in June. She could not have said what he looked like because she never looked at him. But he was yellow and blue somehow and most boys were red and black. He was also smooth and most boys were rough. Somehow, Lorraine felt all right with him in the same way she felt all right with her dad.

Art was nice anyway. You splashed about with water and you made pretty patterns. Miss Crosby, her teacher, often got cross in the Friday art lessons but Lorraine understood that. It was because Miss Crosby was young and new and there were thirty of them in the class and there was only one of her and the boys sometimes behaved badly. Lorraine liked Miss Crosby. But not as much as she liked Thomas Baldwin.

Today's Friday art lesson is more than usually lovely. Today they are making patterns in twos. Some of the boys were silly about that, as usual. But not Thomas Baldwin.

'What colours do you want to do?' he asks her, in that serious way he has.

'Yellow and blue,' she says. And she wants to say 'like you'. But she doesn't. Though she keeps saying 'Yellow and blue like you,' over and over again in her head because the rhyme makes her happy. She and Thomas Baldwin work steadily and quietly together while most of the others throw paint and water at each other or talk and scream. 'Yellow and blue like you.' Paint, paint. Happy.

When Miss gets to them she has that high voice she sometimes has at the end of the week. 'Finished, Miss,' says Lorraine and waits anxiously for the expected praise, which, when withheld, leads to tears.

'That's very good, Lorraine Pitcher and Thomas Baldwin,' says Miss Crosby. 'Now empty your water and start another one.'

Miss Crosby moves distractedly across the classroom to break up a water fight.

'Come on,' Lorraine says to Thomas. She gets up and crosses the classroom, carrying the dirty water in a jam jar. When she reaches the sink she knows, she just *knows*, that he has followed her. She looks round breathlessly. And he has. He has.

Lorraine throws the dirty water into the sink, sighing the way her mother does when she does the housework. She fills the jam jar with clean water. 'Come on,' she says again to Thomas Baldwin and again Thomas Baldwin follows her.

In later life Lorraine sometimes wondered if she would have been *Mrs* Baldwin if she had got back to her seat without incident. But life had another path for her. She tripped over Peter Robinson, who for some reason was lying on the floor, went down with a bang and spilled the water all down the front of her dress. She burst into tears in an untidy wet heap on the floor.

'Silly girl,' said Thomas Baldwin, as he stepped carefully over her. As the bell went, he walked into the playground and out of her life.

Choose the correct answers. There is sometimes more than one correct answer.

1   Who did Lorraine like?

    a) Her dad.

    b) Thomas Baldwin.

    c) Miss Crosby.

    d) Peter Robinson.

2   Who and/or what was yellow and blue?

    a) Thomas Baldwin – he had blonde hair and blue eyes.

    b) Miss Crosby.

    c) The jam jar.

    d) The pattern.

3   Why did Lorraine like art?

    a) Because she liked Miss Crosby.

    b) Because she sat next to Thomas Baldwin.

    c) Because she splashed about with water and made pretty patterns.

    d) Because there were water fights.

4   What did Lorraine like about Thomas Baldwin?

    a) He made her feel all right.

    b) He was serious.

    c) She would have been his wife.

    d) He stepped over her carefully.

5   What went wrong in the story?

    a) Lorraine tripped and fell over.

    b) Lorraine spilled water down the front of her dress.

    c) The bell went and Thomas Baldwin went into the playground.

    d) Thomas Baldwin called her a silly girl.

# 50 Comedy

This is an extract from *The Day an Alien Scored for Leyton Orient* by Gavin Ray.

XJ7 (his friends call him XJ) comes from the most advanced civilization the universe has ever seen. But even they get problems. On this particular day his one-man spaceship developed the only problem he couldn't repair with his mind. He was three universes away from home, too far away to call for help. He was near the planet Earth and he had to land.

Now, XJ7 was five metres tall, bright green, had six arms, ten legs and a fully computerized brain. So he knew people would notice him. Therefore, he had to take the identity of someone from the planet Earth, then land and then get the computer parts. Even on Earth they had the parts he needed.

His computerized mind checked the identity of every person on the planet in less than one nano-second. He took the identity of Jimmy Pearce, a striker with the Third Division Football Team, Leyton Orient. With one wave of one of his six arms, XJ7 put the real Pearce to sleep in his flat. When Pearce woke up, he would remember nothing. XJ7 looked down at himself. He looked like a human being in a red football shirt and white shorts. He had a number nine on his back.

His computerized mind was giving him more and more information. This was an important game for Leyton Orient. If they won, promotion from Division Three to Division Two was certain. He, Jimmy Pearce, wasn't a very good striker. Only two goals in twelve games so far this season. The last thing XJ7 did before landing his spaceship was to press a button to make himself a better footballer. A much better footballer ...

'You're late! Where on earth have you been?'

The data came through into XJ7's computer-mind. The man speaking to him was Dan Grimes, the Chief Coach of Leyton Orient. He must reply.

'I am an alien from the planet Gorb,' said Jimmy Pearce. 'I need computer parts to return to my home planet.'

Dan Grimes's eyes opened wide. 'Pearce! Have you gone mad?'

XJ7 thought hard. He searched his computer-mind. He was telling the truth. There was a fault somewhere. Ah, now the data was coming through properly. He nodded and started again.

'Just my little joke, Dan,' he said. 'Don't you worry about a thing. Promotion to Division Two is as good as ours.'

XJ7 ran out on to the pitch with his teammates. The crowd (10,764) roared.

Much later, back on the planet Gorb, XJ7 worked out what happened next. But he noticed nothing at the time. When the spaceship landed he had made himself a better footballer. But he had pressed the button a bit too hard ...

Jimmy Pearce got the ball and nobody from the opposing team – the unfortunate Sidcup United – could get it back from him. They tackled him, they threw themselves at him, they joined arms and lined up in front of him ... nothing worked. Pearce scored ten times in the first fifteen minutes. The half-time score of Leyton Orient 35 Sidcup United 2 is still a happy memory for Orient fans. But of course it couldn't last.

At half time Pearce failed a drugs test. He found a computer shop, bought the parts he needed and went home. The Football League ordered the match replayed. When Leyton Orient won 2-0 there was a huge cheer from the most advanced civilization the universe has ever seen.

First reading. True or false?

1  XJ7 phoned the planet Gorb and asked for help. _____

2  XJ7 took another identity because he looked very different to people on earth. _____

3  XJ7 landed his spaceship because he needed a new part for it. _____

4  XJ7 found information about Jimmy Pearce after he landed his spaceship. _____

5  Leyton Orient play in red and white. _____

6  XJ7 killed the real Jimmy Pearce. _____

7  XJ7 made himself a better footballer than Jimmy Pearce. _____

8  Dan Grimes did not notice anything different about Jimmy Pearce. _____

9  XJ7 played as well as the real Jimmy Pearce would have done. _____

10 XJ7 as Jimmy Pearce played the whole game against Sidcup United. _____

11 The match against Sidcup United was played twice. _____

12 XJ7 got home to Gorb OK. _____

Second reading. Put the events in the order they happened.

a  XJ7 told Dan Grimes the truth about himself. _____

b  XJ7 went home. _____

c  XJ7 played very well against Sidcup United. _____

d  XJ7 failed a drugs test. _____

e  XJ7 got the parts he needed for his spaceship. _____

f  XJ7's spaceship developed a problem. _____

g  XJ7 took the identity of Jimmy Pearce. _____

h  The match Leyton Orient vs Sidcup United was played again and Leyton Orient won. _____

i  XJ7 made himself a better footballer than Jimmy Pearce. _____

# 51 Headlines

**A**

### Earthquake leaves hundreds dead

An earthquake in Yarmistan, near Armenia, left hundreds dead in the early hours of this morning. Dozens more are feared trapped in collapsed buildings.

**B**

### No change in interest rates, says Chancellor

The Chancellor of the Exchequer, Peter Malahide, yesterday denied rumours of an interest rate rise. 'There is no reason for interest rates to change at the moment,' he said.

**C**

### Jimmy Pearce for AC Milan?

Leyton Orient striker Jimmy Pearce has again been linked with a dream move to Italian giants AC Milan. Pearce, who has been unable to recover the form that led to his amazing tally of goals in the first half of the abandoned game against Sidcup, said, 'It's news to me.'

**D**

### Crime rate up for third year running

Crimes reported to police rose for the third year running in figures released by the Home Office late last night.
The only good news was on car crime and burglary, both significantly down.

**E**

### Mayor makes stand against GM crops

The Major of Oldchester, Mr Timothy Deal, 56, yesterday threw his weight behind the growing numbers who have reservations about GM crops.
Speaking from his home in Oldchester, Mr Deal said that more research is needed.

**F**

### French ballet to visit Britain

The distinguished Ballet de Rouen is to pay its first visit to Britain in over twenty years.
The company will dance at the Littleborough Arts Festival for two weeks next May, announced a delighted Mayor of Littleborough, Tony Fitch.

---

A headline gives as much information about the story as possible in a short space. The newspaper story is then summarized in the first paragraph after the headline. The next paragraph usually contains important information too.

Headlines are different from most other forms of English. They often use the present simple tense for past time (see headline A). They often use *is to* or *to* for the future (see F).

Articles and the verb *to be* are often left out (see D).

*GM* = Genetically Modified (plants that have been changed by people)

First reading. The headlines and the opening lines of the stories are from a British newspaper. Answer the questions.

1    Which headline is from the sports page? _____

2    Which headline is from the foreign news page? _____

3    Which headline is from the arts page? _____

4    Which headlines are from the home news page? _____

5    Which headline is from the finance page? _____

Second reading. Answer these questions about the stories with *Yes* or *No*.

**A**

1    Do we know that dozens of people are trapped? _____

2    Does 'left hundreds dead' mean 'killed hundreds'? _____

**B**

3    Are interest rates going up? _____

4    Are people saying that interest rates will go up? _____

**C**

5    Is Jimmy Pearce definitely going to AC Milan? _____

6    Has Jimmy Pearce played as well again as he did in the first half against Sidcup? _____

**D**

7    Is the crime rate definitely going up? _____

8    Is the crime rate for all crimes going up? _____

**E**

9    Did the Mayor say he was against GM crops? _____

10    Was the Mayor speaking at a meeting? _____

**F**

11    Is the ballet company definitely coming to Littleborough? _____

12    Has the ballet company been to Britain before? _____

# 52 Diary

This is an extract from the diary of Stephen Montague, aged 22.

## Monday September 1

First day in a new job! I mean, it's supposed to be such an important day in your life. And I've looked forward to it ... How long? Well, right through the accountancy course at college if not before. So Day 1 the boss says he's got some bad news. The Gloucester branch is relocating up north. Some existing staff are going, some aren't. Most aren't. Well, cheers Mr Bradley. Then he tells me he tried to stop Head Office in London appointing me, but it just went through before the decision was taken.

## Tuesday September 2

The atmosphere is really terrible. Nobody's doing any work. There are union meetings. Everybody's talking about who it will be – who gets the chop and who stays. People are nice to me, but I think that's because they think I've had it. Last in first out and all that. The afternoon with Josie was nice though. She's supposed to be showing me the ropes but we were nattering the whole time about our past lives.

## Wednesday September 3

There have been some acts of vandalism. Somebody's blocked the toilets and the heating was jammed on for a couple of hours. Bradley called Security and we've got these private security guards in the toilets now. Great! The first people got redundancy notices today. Nobody I know, but then I hardly know anybody. I'm fed up. I'm going to ask Josie out for a drink. She can only say no.

## Thursday September 4

Things are looking up. Josie asked me for a drink! Then she cancelled with loads of apologies but we're going tomorrow. I don't know if anybody else is going or not. She's a bit older than me. I think she's twenty-eight. I've always liked older women! I actually did some work today. Did a few spreadsheets on possible new business in accident insurance. Josie checked it, which she didn't have to. I mean I really really like ... No, pack it in. See how it goes tomorrow.

## Friday September 5

Friday – relocating, so's Josie. Am in love. No time for diary.

First reading. Choose the best answer, a or b.

**1**  Does Stephen work at Head Office?

a) Yes          b) No

**2**  How many acts of vandalism does Stephen mention?

a) Two          b) Three

**3**  Did Stephen get a redundancy notice?

a) Yes          b) No

**4**  Did Stephen ask Josie out for a drink?

a) Yes          b) No

**5**  Who should 'pack it in'?

a) Josie          b) Stephen

Second reading. Match the phrases (1–8) with the meanings (a–h).

**1**  gets the chop

**2**  had it

**3**  showing me the ropes

**4**  nattering

**5**  fed up

**6**  looking up

**7**  loads of

**8**  pack it in

**a**  is made redundant

**b**  talking

**c**  unhappy

**d**  a lot of

**e**  getting better

**f**  explaining what to do

**g**  stop it

**h**  no chance

# 53 How to survive an earthquake

### 1. If you are indoors, stay there!

Get under a desk or a table and hold onto it, or move into a doorway. The next best place is in a hallway or against an inside wall. Stay away from windows and heavy furniture or appliances. Get out of the kitchen, which is a dangerous place. Do not run downstairs or rush outside while the building is shaking or while there is danger of falling and hurting yourself or being hit by falling glass or debris.

### 2. If you are outside, get into the open.

Get away from buildings, power lines, chimneys and anything else that might fall on you.

### 3. If you are driving, stop carefully.

Move your car as far out of traffic as possible. Do not stop on or under a bridge or under trees, streetlights, power lines or signs. Stay inside your car until the shaking stops.

### 4. After the quake stops, check for injuries and apply the necessary first aid or seek help.

Do not attempt to move seriously injured people. Cover them with blankets and get medical help for serious injuries.

### 5. Check for hazards.

■ If you can, put on a pair of sturdy thick-soled shoes (in case you step on broken glass, debris, etc.).

■ Put out fires in your home or neighborhood immediately.

■ Shut off the gas if broken pipes or odor cause you to suspect a gas leak.

■ Do not use matches, lighters, camp stoves, barbecues, electrical equipment or appliances until you are sure there are no gas leaks.

■ Shut off electrical power if there is any damage to house wiring.

### 6. Check food and water supplies.

Do not eat or drink anything from open containers near broken glass. If the power is off, plan meals to use up frozen foods or foods that will spoil quickly. Food in the freezer should be good for at least twenty-four to forty-eight hours. If the water is off, you can drink from water heaters, melted ice cubes or canned vegetables. Avoid drinking from swimming pools.

### 7. Be prepared for aftershocks.

Another quake, larger or smaller, may follow. Use your telephone only for a medical or fire emergency – you could tie up lines needed for emergency response.

*Taken from The Worst Case Scenario Survival Handbook – Piven & Borgenicht (Chronicle Books)*

Read the information. Tick (✓) if these people are doing the right thing during an earthquake and put a cross (✗) if they are not.

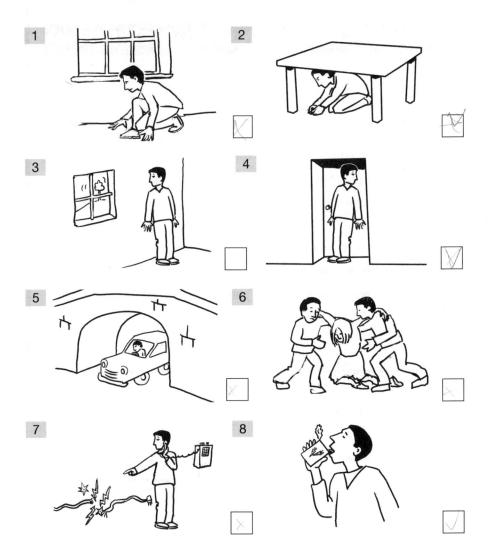

🔍 *debris* = Here, anything falling after the earthquake, although debris can mean the remains of anything broken down or destroyed.
American English
*streetlights* = street lights, two words in British English, also called lamp posts
*neighborhood* = neighbourhood in British English
*odor* = odour (a bad smell) in British English

# 54 Recipe

---

## FRUITY CHICKEN AND RICE POT

### Ingredients

| | |
|---|---|
| 1 x 15ml | tablespoon vegetable oil |
| 325g | chicken, cut (1) _____ |
| 1 | medium sized onion, thinly (2) _____ |
| 1 | medium sized red pepper, finely chopped |
| 1 | bay leaf |
| $\frac{1}{2}$ x 5ml | teaspoon ground mixed (3) _____ |
| 397g | can chopped tomatoes |
| 225ml | chicken stock |
| 50g | green split peas, rinse and boil (4) _____, drain |
| 125g | white or brown long grain (5) _____ |
| 220g | can pineapple chunks in juice, drained |

---

Read *Ingredients* and fill in the missing words.

| | | | | |
|---|---|---|---|---|
| for ten minutes | into small cubes | rice | sliced | spices |

## FRUITY CHICKEN AND RICE POT

### Method

- Heat the oil in (1) _____, add the chicken and onion and fry over a medium heat (2) _____, stirring continuously.

- Add the red pepper and continue (3) _____ for 2–3 minutes.

- Stir in the remaining (4) _____ , except the pineapple.

- Cover and simmer for 25–30 minutes.

- Remove the bay leaf.

- Stir in the pineapple and heat (5) _____ for 5–10 minutes.

- Serve with seasonal vegetables or fresh, crusty (6) _____ .

Read *Method* and fill in the missing words.

| | | | |
|---|---|---|---|
| a large saucepan | bread | cooking | for five minutes |
| | gently | ingredients | |

*simmer* = keep just below boiling point

*bay leaf* = a leaf added for flavour while cooking

*ground* = reduced to a fine powder

*chopped* = cut into small pieces that are not all the same size

*sliced* = cut into thin slices

# 55 Formal letter 3: from the police

---

 **WESSEX POLICE**

Camera Enforcement Office
Bragton Police Station
High Street
Bragton
Wessex
WE12 9AB

RICHARD ARTHUR PITT
10 RAGLAN ROAD
SOUTHWICH
WESSEX, WE5 7RJ

An enforcement camera at B1013 Heston Road near the Slipton Roundabout, SOUTHWICH, recorded that on 21/06/2001 at 09:31 a vehicle, registration number R231 DRT, committed the offence of excess speed.

The law allows you to pay a fine of £40 and have your driving licence endorsed with 3 penalty points if you pay the fine within 28 days. (The fine must be paid in full and cannot be paid in instalments.)

But if your driving licence has been endorsed with 9 or more penalty points in the last 3 years, you could be disqualified from driving and you cannot pay a fine and have more points added to your licence.

**YOU MUST COMPLY FULLY WITH THIS OFFER OTHERWISE COURT PROCEEDINGS WILL BE COMMENCED AGAINST YOU.**

**EXTENSIONS TO THE 28 DAYS WILL NOT BE GRANTED.**

---

If you get twelve penalty points on your driving licence in three years in Britain, you lose the licence for a period of time and you cannot drive. You get penalty points for things like speeding and driving through a red light. When you get penalty points, these are written on your driving licence. In other words your licence is endorsed.

First reading. Which summary has no mistakes, a or b?

**a**  This is a formal printed notice from the police which is sent to anyone whose car has been photographed by speed cameras (enforcement cameras). It says that the person driving the car must pay £40 and have three to six points put on their driving licence. The driver must pay within 28 days.

**b**  This is a formal printed notice from the police which is sent to anyone whose car has been photographed by speed cameras (enforcement cameras.) It says that the person driving the car will be taken to court (prosecuted) unless they accept a Fixed Penalty of a £40 fine and three penalty points put on their driving licence. But if the driver already has nine points or more on the licence, the offer of a Fixed Penalty can't be taken and the driver will probably lose his driving licence for a time.

Second reading. Choose the best answer, a or b.

**1**  Who is this letter from?

a) The police          b) Richard Arthur Pitt

**2**  Can the driver pay a fine and not go to court?

a) Yes

b) Yes, unless he has nine or more points on his licence

**3**  Can the fine be paid at £10 a week for four weeks.

a) Yes          b) No

**4**  What has to be done within twenty-eight days?

a) The licence must be sent and the fine paid.

b) The driver has to enter the points on his licence and go to court.

**5**  What would happen if the driver put the letter away and did nothing?

a) He would just get three to six points on his licence.

b) There would be court proceedings against him.

# 56 Newspaper story 1: events

## EMPTY! – No oil as the first hospitals and schools are hit

**B**RITAIN HAS NEARLY STOPPED TODAY, only the second day of the oil crisis. Despite the warning given by Prime Minister Tony Blair, many of Britain's oil refineries are still blocked by lorries, tractors and taxis.

Lorry drivers angry at the price of petrol have again stopped petrol tankers from leaving oil refineries in Wales, the north-west and Essex. The drivers are angry at petrol prices. At 80p per litre Britain has the highest prices in Europe and 60.82p of the price goes to the government in tax.

'I employ twenty people and I'm going out of business,' says haulage contractor Jim Sowerbutts of Lincoln, one of the people blocking the Immingham refinery on the east coast. 'We cannot make a living with petrol at these prices. It's impossible. It makes goods dearer for the consumer. And Britain is an oil producer. It's mad.'

Britain has run out of petrol very quickly. Today well over 1,000 of Britain's 8,000 filling stations ran dry and even more are out of unleaded petrol – the most popular choice. Among those affected today:

● *Hospitals are running out of beds because patients cannot get home either by ambulance or by taxi.*

● *Operations are being postponed because only nurses who live within walking distance of hospital or who use public transport can get in.*

● *There are fears that hospitals will run out of blood.*

● *Supermarkets report that people are buying more tinned goods – stockpiling in case food cannot be delivered.*

● *Some areas of the country, such as Cumbria in the north-west, have almost no public transport services. They are now virtually cut off from the rest of the country and there are fears for food supplies in this and similar areas.*

In a statement yesterday Tony Blair said that however strongly people felt about petrol prices this was not the way to get them down. He said that no government could give in to pressure like this. He explained that recent rises in petrol prices were due to an increase in crude oil prices (to 15.46p per litre), not an increase in government tax.

He then said that Britain would be 'on the way back to normal' within twenty-four hours.

**We shall see!**

---

*hit* = affected (newspaper language)

*fears* = people are afraid that (newspaper language)

*haulage contractor* = firms that deliver other firms' goods by lorry.

*filling stations* = petrol stations

*stockpiling* = buying something you don't need in case there is an emergency.

Choose the best sentence completion, a or b.

1   The oil crisis started
   a) yesterday.
   b) today.

2   The people blocking the oil refineries are
   a) haulage contractors and taxi drivers.
   b) haulage contractors, taxi drivers and farmers.

3   Petrol in Britain costs
   a) 80p per litre.
   b) 60.82p per litre.

4   Petrol is so expensive in Britain because of
   a) the price of crude oil.
   b) government tax.

5   Jim Sowerbutts is angry because
   a) goods are dear for the consumer.
   b) he cannot make a living.

6   The number of petrol stations that have no unleaded petrol is
   a) a lot more than 1,000.
   b) not clear from the story but more than 1,000.

7   Hospitals are running out of beds because
   a) patients have to stay there.
   b) patients are too ill to go home.

8   Hospitals
   a) have run out of blood.
   b) may run out of blood.

9   Supermarkets
   a) are not selling food.
   b) are selling more of some types of food.

10  Cumbria is virtually cut off from the rest of the country because
   a) the buses have no petrol.
   b) there are no buses and the cars have no petrol.

11  Tony Blair said that
   a) people had strong feelings.
   b) petrol prices were coming down.

12  Tony Blair also said that he could not give in to pressure because people
   a) feel strongly.
   b) are doing the wrong thing.

13  Tony Blair explained that petrol prices had gone up because
   a) government taxes had gone up.
   b) crude oil prices had gone up.

14  Tony Blair said that Britain would be
   a) back to normal in a day.
   b) starting to get back to normal in a day.

# 57 Newspaper story 2: people

## Newspaper story 1

### Businessman gave waitress $10,000 tip – it's like a fairy story.

British businessman Gordon Williams had a big surprise for a waitress at a bar in New York City. At the end of the evening he left her a tip of $10,000.

The waitress, Gloria Latrobe, was working at Top Club near Times Square in the centre of New York for a few weeks only. She is studying psychology at New York University.

Miss Latrobe said, 'Gordon spent the evening at the club with some friends. It was his last night in New York. We talked a lot. He's interested in psychology, too. He gave me the money to pay for my last year of college.'

And what did she do when she got the tip? Miss Latrobe laughed. 'I called the manager.' The manager of Top Club, Peter Hay, said 'Of course, we thought it was a mistake and the guy wanted to give a $10 tip. We asked him to sign a paper, promising to pay $10,000. He did that.'

'I'm really happy,' said Miss Latrobe. 'It's like a fairy tale, when a prince walks into your life.'

## Newspaper story 2

### I gave waitress that $10,000 tip – and now my wife wants to know why.

Businessman Gordon Williams, who gave a waitress in New York a $10,000 tip, does not have $10,000 in his account. His bank will not pay the cheque.

'I just want this to go away,' says unhappy Gordon Williams. 'My wife wants to know why I did it. Well, I don't remember doing it at all. The bar has a paper that I signed, so it must be true, but I don't remember doing it.'

Unfortunately for Mr Williams, who has two children, the story will not go away yet.

Gloria Latrobe has been on coast-to-coast television in the US, telling the story again and again. The day after she got the tip, Miss Latrobe described Mr Williams as 'a very nice English gentleman.' Even now she says, 'I hope his family isn't angry with him.'

But there is a happy ending to the story after all. Top Club in New York were so pleased that the club's name was in every newspaper in Britain and the United States that they have given Gloria Latrobe the $10,000 to pay for her last year at NYU.

First reading. Tick (✓) the person or people who ...

|  | Gordon Williams | Gloria Latrobe | Peter Hay/ Top Club |
|---|---|---|---|
| 1 gave a big tip |  |  |  |
| 2 worked at a club for a few weeks |  |  |  |
| 3 is a student |  |  |  |
| 4 worked at a club all the time |  |  |  |
| 5 are interested in psychology |  |  |  |
| 6 called the manager |  |  |  |
| 7 signed a paper |  |  |  |
| 8 doesn't remember giving a big tip |  |  |  |
| 9 has two children |  |  |  |
| 10 wants it all to go away |  |  |  |
| 11 was on television |  |  |  |
| 12 paid $10,000 |  |  |  |

Second reading. Put these events in the order that they happened.

a   Gordon's bank won't pay the cheque. _____

b   Gordon signed a paper. _____

c   Top Club paid Gloria $10,000. _____

d   Peter thought the tip was a mistake. _____

e   Gloria worked at a nightclub. _____

f   Gordon gave Gloria a tip. _____

# 58 Newspaper story 3: sport

# They're off!

Sydney 2000, the long-awaited Millenium Olympic Games, started here in Sydney yesterday. It is HUGE. It is HERE. And it is OURS.

Australians in every corner of the land felt proud as Aboriginal runner Cathy Freeman, who won the 400 metres silver medal in Atlanta four years ago, held up the famous Olympic torch in the opening ceremony at the 110,000-seat Olympic Stadium.

And our pride grew as thirteen-year-old Nikki Webster sang *Under Southern Skies*. And when the tiny figure in her pink dress sang the last line – 'Every child can be a hero if the world can live as one.' – we all felt hope and optimism and we make no apology to anyone for that.

Our Games has 10,000 athletes competing in 28 sports. We have nearly 300 events at 36 venues watched by 250,000 spectators and a predicted audience of 3.5 billion TV viewers worldwide. The 27th Olympics is the biggest yet and every one of us hopes it will be the best.

And who's the best and brightest of our medal hopes? The Sydney Globe nominates the Torpedo – seventeen-year-old Ian Thorpe, the local boy from right here in Sydney. The boy who brought the glory back to Australian swimming is in with a shout for four gold medals: in the 200m and 400m freestyle and the 4 x 100m and 4 x 400m relays.

Thorpe, you will remember, was the youngest Australian since the 1950s to swim for our country when he represented Australia at the age of fourteen. Since then he's broken 10 world records. Competitors like Thorpe are what the Olympics is all about. He laughs when people put his success down to his admittedly enormous hands and feet. He puts it all down to hard work. He starts his training at 4.15 a.m.

Where else can we look for success? Well, tomorrow 15,000 people will gather at the State Hockey Centre at Olympic Park to see if our women's hockey team can take the gold medal for the third time in four Olympics, as they are expected to do. In seven fantastic years under coach Ric Charlesworth the Hockeyroos have won 191 games and lost just 24. Our team are in Pool A along with Argentina, Great Britain, South Korea and Spain.

Among the runners ...

relay = four runners or swimmers run or swim as a team in the race

venue = where a sports event takes place

freestyle = a swimming event where the swimmers can use any style, but usually swim front crawl, swimming face down and putting one arm into the water at a time

Hockeyroos = nickname of the Australian women's hockey team

in with a shout = has a chance

Pool A = Group A

First reading. Are these definite (write D) or possible (write P)?

1   Cathy Freeman's silver medal _____

2   The 10,000 athletes _____

3   The TV audience of 3.5 billion _____

4   The 27th Olympics is the biggest yet. _____

5   The 27th Olympics is the best yet. _____

6   Ian Thorpe's four gold medals _____

7   Ian Thorpe's ten world records _____

8   The Australian women's hockey team's two gold medals _____

9   The Australian women's hockey team's three gold medals. _____

10  The Australian women's hockey team's 191 wins in seven years

    _____

Second reading. Match the beginning of these sentences (1–6) with the ends (a–f).

1   Australians felt proud when

2   Australians make no apology for

3   Australians hope that

4   The *Sydney Globe* believes that

5   Ian Thorpe represented Australia

6   The Australian women's hockey team

a   the 27th Olympics will be the best.

b   Ian Thorpe is Australia's brightest medal hope.

c   is expected to win a third gold medal.

d   at the age of fourteen.

e   feeling hope and optimism.

f   Cathy Freeman held up the Olympic torch.

# 59 Encyclopaedia entry: a 20th century painter

This is taken from *The Encyclopaedia of 20th Century Art*.

## Franz Marc

*Biography*

Franz Moritz Wilhelm Marc was born on 8 February 1880 in Munich, Germany. He was the second son of the Munich landscape painter Wilhelm Marc and his wife Sophie. After deciding not to become a priest he studied art in Munich but broke off his studies after a visit to Paris in 1903 where he was fascinated by French Impressionism, though he disagreed with it. In 1907 he married Marie Schnur, also a Munich painter, who had an illegitimate child with an earlier partner. She and Marc divorced in 1908. An early painting *Schlick, the dog, jumping* was a Christmas present to his mother in that year. In 1910 Marc joined a group of painters based in Munich called *The Blue Rider*, whose best known member was the Russian-born Wassily Kandinsky. In 1911 he married another Munich painter called Maria Franck in London. On 4 March 1916 Marc was killed at the battle of Verdun.

Marc's early painting and drawing were realistic studies of horses, in the style he had learned at the Academy in Munich. He was particularly interested in animals moving, at this time. The early oil painting, *Schlick, the dog, jumping*, belongs to this period. He was also interested in landscape from an early age. But when he joined *The Blue Rider* group he became fascinated by colour. From then on he painted animals, especially horses, as part of the landscape. In the beautiful *Horse in the Landscape* (1910) the horse is not moving. It is part of a beautiful, mainly yellow and green, landscape. The lines of the horse and the lines of the landscape are one.

In *Horse in the Landscape* the horse was still its 'natural' colour – brown. But in 1911 Marc painted the first of a series of paintings called *Blue Horse*. The daring idea was that this particular horse's true colour was blue because blue was the colour of strength, dignity and courage. Blue, for Marc, was the masculine colour. The feminine colour was yellow and in 1912 Marc painted *The Little Yellow Horses*. Three beautiful, graceful yellow horses are again part of the landscape, totally at one with it.

First reading. Match 1–11 with a–k.

| | | | |
|---|---|---|---|
| **1** | Wilhelm Marc | **a** | a painting painted in 1911 |
| **2** | Sophie Marc | **b** | a painter and Marc's second wife |
| **3** | Marie Schnur | **c** | a painter and Marc's first wife |
| **4** | Schlick | **d** | Franz Marc's mother |
| **5** | Wassily Kandinsky | **e** | a painting of a brown horse |
| **6** | Maria Franck | **f** | a painting in the colour Marc thought was feminine |
| **7** | Verdun | **g** | a group of painters in Munich |
| **8** | *The Blue Rider* | **h** | the place where Marc was killed |
| **9** | *Horse in the Landscape* | **i** | a painter in the same group as Marc |
| **10** | *Blue Horse* | **j** | a dog |
| **11** | *The Little Yellow Horses* | **k** | Franz Marc's father |

Second reading. Put these events in the order that they happened.

**a** He was no longer interested in movement, more in the colour of the landscape and animals as part of the landscape. _____

**b** He thought of a system of colour for animals. _____

**c** He painted realistic studies of horses as they really were. _____

**d** He disagreed with French Impressionism. _____

**e** He became interested in animals moving. _____

*landscape* = a painting of scenery or buildings
*an illegitimate child* = the parents were not married.
*French Impressionism* = a very influential style of painting that started in France. The best known French impressionist was probably Claude Monet (1840–1926). Others were Paul Cézanne (1839–1906), Camille Pissarro (1831–1903) and Georges Seurat (1859–1891).

# 60 Ideas

## Charles Darwin (1809–1882)

Before Darwin's book *On the Origin of Species* (1859) people believed that everything in the world was created at the same time. They believed that every animal and plant had always been the same and had not changed in any way.

*Fossils in a rock*

Then Darwin looked at rocks. In the rocks were fossils – life 'frozen' in the rock. The newest fossils were at the top of the rock. But as Darwin looked under them he found older and older life forms, until at the bottom of the rock he found animals that no longer lived in the world at all.

The old fossils, deep in the rock, had changed into the newer fossils at the top. This slow change was known as evolution. All species, that is all plants and animals, evolved – changed. Most famously, he said that our species, *homo sapiens*, man, had evolved from monkeys.

*Darwin thought that man evolved from monkeys.*

Darwin also asked himself why evolution happened in one direction and not another. His answer was an idea called 'the survival of the fittest'. For example, the giraffe with the longest neck would survive because it can reach the tops of trees and so it can find food. Because it can find food, that giraffe would live long enough to have young giraffes, which would be born with long necks.

*A giraffe reaches the top branches of the tree with its long neck.*

*The young giraffe has a long neck, too.*

First reading. Match the beginning of these sentences (1–6) with the ends (a–f).

| | | | |
|---|---|---|---|
| 1 | Before Darwin's book people believed | a | were at the bottom. |
| 2 | The newer fossils | b | man evolving from monkeys. |
| 3 | Older fossils | c | into the newer fossils. |
| 4 | The older fossils had changed | d | were at the top of the rock. |
| 5 | An example of evolution is | e | every animal came into being at the same time. |
| 6 | An example of 'survival of the fittest' is | f | the long necks of giraffes. |

Second reading. Answer these questions with *one* word.

1  Who wrote *On the Origin of Species?* _____

2  Where were the newer fossils, at the top or the bottom of the rock? _____

3  What is slow change called? _____

4  Darwin believed that our species had evolved from what?

_____

5  Which animal did Darwin use as an example of 'survival of the fittest'? _____

6  Which part of this animal is important for the idea of 'survival of the fittest'? _____

# Answers

## Section 1: Messages

### Test 1

| | |
|---|---|
| 1 c, e | 7 e |
| 2 e | 8 a, d, f |
| 3 c | 9 b |
| 4 b | 10 f |
| 5 a | 11 e, f |
| 6 d | |

### Test 2
First reading

| | |
|---|---|
| 1 e | 4 a |
| 2 f | 5 c |
| 3 d | 6 b |

Second reading

| | |
|---|---|
| 1 a | 4 b |
| 2 b | 5 a |
| 3 a | 6 b |

### Test 3

| | | |
|---|---|---|
| 1 b | 6 g | 11 h |
| 2 i | 7 k | 12 f |
| 3 m | 8 j | 13 a |
| 4 c | 9 d | |
| 5 l | 10 e | |

### Test 4

| | |
|---|---|
| 1 ✗ | 5 ✗ |
| 2 ✗ | 6 ✗ |
| 3 ✓ | 7 ✓ |
| 4 ✗ | 8 ✗ |

### Test 5

| | | |
|---|---|---|
| 1 a | 4 b | 7 b |
| 2 a | 5 b | 8 a |
| 3 b | 6 a | 9 b |

### Test 6
First reading

| | |
|---|---|
| Picture 1 – 2 | Picture 4 – 6 |
| Picture 2 – 4 | Picture 5 – 1 |
| Picture 3 – 7 | Picture 6 – 3 |

Second reading

1 £13.89
2 £11.99
3 £10.14

### Test 7
First reading

| | |
|---|---|
| 1 enter | 5 teachers |
| 2 reviews | 6 categories |
| 3 prizes | 7 form |
| 4 winners | |

Second reading

| | |
|---|---|
| 1 twelve | 4 books |
| 2 review | 5 no |
| 3 five | |

### Test 8
First reading

| | | |
|---|---|---|
| 1 g | 4 c | 7 d |
| 2 f | 5 e | 8 h |
| 3 b | 6 a | |

Second reading

| | |
|---|---|
| 1 b | 3 b |
| 2 a | 4 a |

### Test 9
The note

| | | |
|---|---|---|
| 1 T | 4 T | 7 F |
| 2 T | 5 F | 8 T |
| 3 F | 6 T | |

The memo

| | | |
|---|---|---|
| 1 F | 4 F | 7 F |
| 2 T | 5 T | 8 F |
| 3 F | 6 T | |

### Test 10
First reading
b

Second reading

1 Gavin
2 Christine and David
3 Maureen and Clive
4 Christine and David
5 Gavin
6 Maureen and Clive
7 Gavin and Melanie
8 Gavin
9 Maureen and Clive
10 Melanie
11 Christine and David

**Test 11**
| | | | |
|---|---|---|---|
| 1 | c | 3 | d |
| 2 | a | 4 | b |

## Section 2: People

**Test 12**
| | | | | | |
|---|---|---|---|---|---|
| 1 | c | 4 | a | 7 | b |
| 2 | a | 5 | a | 8 | c |
| 3 | b | 6 | c | 9 | a |

**Test 13**
First reading
| 1 | Neither | 7 | New Boy |
|---|---|---|---|
| 2 | Worried Girl | 8 | Worried Girl |
| 3 | Both | 9 | New Boy |
| 4 | New Boy | 10 | Both |
| 5 | New Boy | 11 | Both |
| 6 | New Boy | | |

Second reading
| 1 | furniture | 4 | starving |
|---|---|---|---|
| 2 | ridiculous | 5 | nervous |
| 3 | fry up | | |

**Test 14**
1 Outgoing
2 Check this out
3 Summer fun!/A good catch
4 Outgoing
5 Check this out
6 Summer fun!
7 Summer fun!
8 1
9 2
10 2
11 1
12 1
13 3
14 1

**Test 15**
First reading
| 1 | C | 6 | C |
|---|---|---|---|
| 2 | B | 7 | B, C |
| 3 | B, C, D | 8 | A, B |
| 4 | A, C, E, F | 9 | B |
| 5 | A, E | 10 | C |

Second reading
| 1 | h | 5 | f |
|---|---|---|---|
| 2 | c | 6 | e |
| 3 | b | 7 | a |
| 4 | g | 8 | d |

**Test 16**
First reading
a in reply to
b at present
c In your advertisement
d is required
e enclosing
f to attend for interview

Second reading
| a | 3 | d | 6 |
|---|---|---|---|
| b | 4 | e | 2 |
| c | 1 | f | 5 |

**Test 17**
Aries: square, place, no
Taurus: pleasant, until, unpleasant
Gemini: for, point, of
Cancer: welcome, you, the
Leo: your, fruit, on

**Test 18**
First reading
Jane Peters
| 1 | F | 3 | F |
|---|---|---|---|
| 2 | T | 4 | T |

Arthur Sugden
| 1 | T | 3 | T |
|---|---|---|---|
| 2 | F | 4 | T |

Dickie Gallagher
| 1 | F | 3 | T |
|---|---|---|---|
| 2 | T | 4 | F |

Second reading
Jane: picture 2
Arthur: picture 3
Dickie: picture 6

**Test 19**
| | | | | | |
|---|---|---|---|---|---|
| 1 | a | 4 | a | 7 | c |
| 2 | c | 5 | b | 8 | b |
| 3 | b | 6 | c | | |

**Test 20**
| | | | | | |
|---|---|---|---|---|---|
| 1 | c | 4 | c | 7 | b |
| 2 | a | 5 | c | 8 | b |
| 3 | b | 6 | b | | |

**Test 21**

First reading – a

Second reading

| | | | |
|---|---|---|---|
| a | 2–1 | e | 1–2 |
| b | 1–2 | f | 1–2 |
| c | 2–1 | g | 2–1 |
| d | 2–1 | h | 1–2 |

**Test 22**

First reading

| | | | | | |
|---|---|---|---|---|---|
| 1 | D | 5 | P | 9 | D |
| 2 | P | 6 | D | 10 | P |
| 3 | P | 7 | D | | |
| 4 | D | 8 | D | | |

Second reading
born 1564
married 1582
had children 1583, 1585
left Stratford 1587
bought New Place 1597
Globe Theatre opened 1599
Globe Theatre burned down 1613
died 1616

**Test 23**

First reading
d, b, a, e, c

Second reading

| | | | |
|---|---|---|---|
| 1 | depot | some | think |
| 2 | never | one | not |
| 3 | with | cowboys | I |

**Test 24**

First reading
2  4  5  6  7

Second reading

| | | | | | |
|---|---|---|---|---|---|
| 1 | e | 4 | f | 7 | d |
| 2 | g | 5 | b | | |
| 3 | c | 6 | a | | |

## Section 3: Places

**Test 25**

First reading

| | | | |
|---|---|---|---|
| 1 | last | 5 | card |
| 2 | staying | 6 | city |
| 3 | million | 7 | together |
| 4 | way | 8 | back |

Second reading

| | | | | | |
|---|---|---|---|---|---|
| 1 | F | 4 | T | 7 | T |
| 2 | F | 5 | F | | |
| 3 | T | 6 | T | | |

**Test 26**

First reading
1  both
2  both
3  both
4  Lakeside Cabins
5  Lakeside Cabins
6  Lakeside Cabins
7  both

Second reading

| | | | | | |
|---|---|---|---|---|---|
| 1 | b | 4 | b | 7 | a |
| 2 | b | 5 | b | | |
| 3 | a | 6 | a | | |

**Test 27**

| | | | | | |
|---|---|---|---|---|---|
| 1 | b | 2 | a | 3 | a |

**Test 28**

First reading
The country: the, countries, boring
The best ski schools: not, don't, don't
Snowboarding: slow
Duty-free shopping: low, a
Andorra facts: currency, sometimes, often

Second reading
2  5  8  11  12  13  15  16

**Test 29**

First reading
2  3  4  7  8  10  11

Second reading

| | | | | | |
|---|---|---|---|---|---|
| 1 | F | 3 | T | 5 | F |
| 2 | F | 4 | T | | |

**Test 30**

First reading
5  3  1  2  6  4

Second reading

| | | | | | |
|---|---|---|---|---|---|
| 1 | c | 3 | a | 5 | d |
| 2 | e | 4 | b | | |

**Test 31**

| | | | | | |
|---|---|---|---|---|---|
| 1 | ✗ | 4 | ✗ | 7 | ✗ |
| 2 | ✗ | 5 | ✓ | 8 | ✗ |
| 3 | ✓ | 6 | ✗ | 9 | ✗ |

## Test 32
First reading
Picture 3

Second reading

| | | |
|---|---|---|
| 1 b | 3 a | 5 b |
| 2 b | 4 b | |

## Test 33

| | | |
|---|---|---|
| 1 a | 5 c | 9 a |
| 2 a | 6 c | 10 a |
| 3 c | 7 a | |
| 4 b | 8 c | |

## Test 34
First reading

| | |
|---|---|
| 1 two | 4 bathroom |
| 2 football | 5 wash |
| 3 yes | 6 walk |

Second reading

| | | | |
|---|---|---|---|
| work | food | houses | countryside |
| mines | greens | cottages | moors |
| comedian | beef | | |
| vicar | fish | | |
| professional footballer | | | |

## Test 35
First reading

| | | |
|---|---|---|
| 1 T | 4 T | 7 T |
| 2 T | 5 T | 8 T |
| 3 T | 6 F | |

Second reading

| | | |
|---|---|---|
| 1 f | 3 d | 5 b |
| 2 a | 4 e | 6 c |

## Section 4: Things

## Test 36

| | |
|---|---|
| 1 F | 6 B, D, F |
| 2 C, D | 7 A, D, F |
| 3 C, E, F | 8 B, C, D |
| 4 D | 9 E |
| 5 B, F | |

## Test 37

| | | |
|---|---|---|
| 1 b, c | 4 a, b | 7 a |
| 2 a, b | 5 c | |
| 3 c | 6 a, b | |

## Test 38
1 a, d, e, f
2 a, d, e, g
3 aF, bF, cF, dF, eF, fF, gT

## Test 39
First reading

| | | |
|---|---|---|
| 1 F | 5 F | 9 T |
| 2 T | 6 T | 10 F |
| 3 F | 7 T | 11 T |
| 4 T | 8 T | 12 T |

Second reading
2, 3, 4, 5

## Test 40
First reading

| | |
|---|---|
| 1 B, C, E | 4 E |
| 2 C, D, F | 5 F |
| 3 A, D, F | |

Second reading
1 participating
2 selected items
3 locally
4 date shown opposite
5 plus £2.95 p&p
6 up to as much as 50%
7 with your order
8 one pair per purchase
9 fully priced
10 between now and 30 September
11 valued customer
12 before the Sale starts to the General Public
14 or

## Test 41
First reading
parts of a computer: loudspeakers, modem, the fan, a scanner
operations: download files, start-up, attach a file
problems: it freezes, it doesn't ... work, it blew up

Second reading

| | | |
|---|---|---|
| 1 c | 3 d | 5 b |
| 2 e | 4 a | |

**Test 42**
First reading
Picture 1 b Picture 3 a
Picture 2 d Picture 4 c

Second reading
1 vest tops
2 sandals
3 vest tops
4 pedal pushers
5 pedal pushers
6 pedal pushers/vest tops
7 pedal pushers
8 black dress
9 black dress

**Test 43**
1 a2 b3 c4 d1
2 c

## Section 5: Fiction

**Test 44**
First reading
1 shoe 5 biscuit
2 night 6 hall
3 funny 7 there
4 knife 8 away

Second reading
1 A and C 2 B 3 D

**Test 45**
About *Teenage Monster*
1 b 2 a 3 a

About *Country Doc*
4 b 5 a 6 a

About *Dino*
7 b 8 a 9 a

**Test 46**
First reading
b

Second reading
1 F 4 T 7 F
2 F 5 T 8 T
3 T 6 T

**Test 47**
1 1 c 4 d
2 e 5 f
3 a 6 b

2 1 e 3 a 5 c
2 f 4 b 6 d

**Test 48**
First reading
1 Yes 3 No 5 Yes
2 Yes 4 Yes 6 No

Second reading
1 h 4 b 7 c
2 a 5 d 8 f
3 g 6 e

**Test 49**
1 a, b, c 4 a, b
2 a, d 5 a, b, d
3 a, b

**Test 50**
First reading
1 F 5 T 9 F
2 T 6 F 10 F
3 T 7 T 11 T
4 F 8 F 12 T

Second reading
f, g, i, a, c, d, e, b, h

## Section 6: Fact

**Test 51**
First reading
1 C 3 F 5 B
2 A 4 D & E

Second reading
1 No 5 No 9 Yes
2 Yes 6 No 10 No
3 No 7 Yes 11 Yes
4 Yes 8 No 12 Yes

## Test 52
First reading

| | | |
|---|---|---|
| 1 b | 3 b | 5 b |
| 2 a | 4 b | |

Second reading

| | | |
|---|---|---|
| 1 a | 4 b | 7 d |
| 2 h | 5 c | 8 g |
| 3 f | 6 e | |

## Test 53

| | |
|---|---|
| Picture 1 ✗ | Picture 5 ✗ |
| Picture 2 ✗ | Picture 6 ✗ |
| Picture 3 ✓ | Picture 7 ✗ |
| Picture 4 ✓ | Picture 8 ✓ |

## Test 54
Ingredients
1 into small cubes
2 sliced
3 spices ·
4 for ten minutes
5 rice

Method
1 a large saucepan
2 for five minutes
3 cooking
4 ingredients
5 gently
6 bread

## Test 55
First reading
b

Second reading

| | | |
|---|---|---|
| 1 a | 3 b | 5 b |
| 2 b | 4 a | |

## Test 56

| | | |
|---|---|---|
| 1 a | 6 b | 11 a |
| 2 b | 7 a | 12 b |
| 3 a | 8 b | 13 b |
| 4 b | 9 b | 14 b |
| 5 b | 10 b | |

## Test 57
First reading
1 Gordon Williams
2 Gloria Latrobe
3 Gloria Latrobe
4 Peter Hay
5 Gordon Williams, Gloria Latrobe
6 Gloria Latrobe
7 Gordon Williams
8 Gordon Williams
9 Gordon Williams
10 Gordon Williams
11 Gloria Latrobe
12 Peter Hay

Second reading
e   f   d   b   a   c

## Test 58
First reading

| | | |
|---|---|---|
| 1 D | 5 P | 9 P |
| 2 D | 6 P | 10 D |
| 3 P | 7 D | |
| 4 D | 8 D | |

Second reading

| | | |
|---|---|---|
| 1 f | 3 a | 5 d |
| 2 e | 4 b | 6 c |

## Test 59
First reading

| | | |
|---|---|---|
| 1 k | 5 i | 9 e |
| 2 d | 6 b | 10 a |
| 3 c | 7 h | 11 f |
| 4 j | 8 g | |

Second reading

| | | |
|---|---|---|
| 1 d | 3 e | 5 c |
| 2 a | 4 b | |

## Test 60
First reading

| | | |
|---|---|---|
| 1 e | 3 a | 5 b |
| 2 d | 4 c | 6 f |

Second reading

| | | |
|---|---|---|
| 1 Darwin | 4 monkeys |
| 2 top | 5 giraffe |
| 3 evolution | 6 neck |

# Test Your way to success in English
## Test Your Vocabulary

0582 45166 3

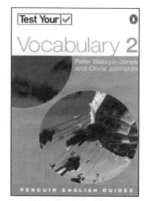

0582 45167 1

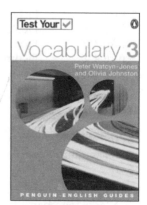

0582 45168 X

0582 45169 8

0582 45170 1

**www.penguinenglish.com**